Neural Networks in Unity

C# Programming for Windows 10

Abhishek Nandy
Manisha Biswas

Apress®

Neural Networks in Unity

Abhishek Nandy
Kolkata, West Bengal, India

Manisha Biswas
North 24 Parganas, West Bengal, India

ISBN-13 (pbk): 978-1-4842-3672-7
https://doi.org/10.1007/978-1-4842-3673-4

ISBN-13 (electronic): 978-1-4842-3673-4

Library of Congress Control Number: 2018951222

Managing Director, Apress Media LLC: Welmoed Spahr
Acquisitions Editor: Celestin Suresh John
Development Editor: Matthew Moodie
Coordinating Editor: Aditee Mirashi

Cover designed by eStudioCalamar

Cover image designed by Freepik (www.freepik.com)

Distributed to the book trade worldwide by Springer Science+Business Media New York, 233 Spring Street, 6th Floor, New York, NY 10013. Phone 1-800-SPRINGER, fax (201) 348-4505, e-mail orders-ny@springer-sbm.com, or visit www.springeronline.com. Apress Media, LLC is a California LLC and the sole member (owner) is Springer Science + Business Media Finance Inc (SSBM Finance Inc). SSBM Finance Inc is a Delaware corporation.

For information on translations, please e-mail rights@apress.com, or visit www.apress.com/rights-permissions.

Apress titles may be purchased in bulk for academic, corporate, or promotional use. eBook versions and licenses are also available for most titles. For more information, reference our Print and eBook Bulk Sales web page at www.apress.com/bulk-sales.

Any source code or other supplementary material referenced by the author in this book is available to readers on GitHub via the book's product page, located at www.apress.com/978-1-4842-3672-7. For more detailed information, please visit www.apress.com/source-code.

Printed on acid-free paper

This book is dedicated to my parents.

—*Abhishek Nandy*

This book is dedicated to my parents and the spirit of Women Techmakers.

—*Manisha Biswas*

Table of Contents

About the Authors

Abhishek Nandy is B.Tech in IT and he is a constant learner. He is a Microsoft MVP for Windows Platform, Intel Black Belt Developer as well as Intel Software Innovator. He has a keen interest in AI, IoT, and game development.

He is currently serving as an Application Architect in an IT firm as well as consulting on AI, IoT and doing projects on AI, ML, and deep learning. He also is an AI trainer, driving the technical part of the Intel AI Student developer program. He was involved in the first Make in India initiative, where he was among top 50 innovators and got trained in IIMA.

Manisha Biswas is B.Tech in Information Technology and currently working as Data Scientist at Prescriber360 in Kolkata, India. She is involved with several areas of technology including Web Development, IoT, Soft Computing, and Artificial Intelligence. She is an Intel Software Innovator and was also awarded the SHRI DEWANG MEHTA IT AWARDS 2016 by NASSCOM, a certificate of excellence for top academic scores. She is the founder of WOMEN IN TECHNOLOGY, Kolkata, a tech community to empower women to learn and explore new technologies. She always likes to invent things, create something new, or to invent a new look for the old things. When not in front of her terminal, she is an explorer, a traveller, a foodie, a doodler, and a dreamer. She is always very passionate to share her knowledge and ideas with others. She is following her passion and doing the same currently by sharing her experiences with the community so that others can learn and give shape to her ideas in a new way. This led her to become Google Women Techmakers Kolkata Chapter Lead.

About the Technical Reviewer

 **Ali Asad** is an avid programmer with experience in various areas, including gameplay programming, custom add-in/tool/plugin development, computation programming, artificial intelligence, consulting, and formulating strategies. His career has covered the life cycle of application across different domains, such as AEC industry and Education.

He authored a book *The C# Programmer's Study Guide (MCSD)*. He's also a *Microsoft Specialist: Programming in C#*. You can learn more about his various other activities at: www.linkedin.com/in/imaliasad/

Introduction

This book is an attempt to cover Unity with an approach to touch machine learning and neural networks.

We have given a brief introduction to useful neural network terminologies to start with.

The attempt has been made to use the new Unity-ML-Agents version 0.3 and clearly construct the process.

What do you need? A basic understanding or fresh approach to cover the Unity engine with respect to ML and Neural Networks. We have kept things simple to adapt.

CHAPTER 1

Neural Network Basics

The evolvement of artificial intelligence, machine learning, and deep learning has made so many people start asking questions about what exactly the process of machine learning actually is?

We found that data scientists, enthusiasts, and developers are very curious to learn how a neural network works for helping artificial intelligence to perform better.

In this chapter, we will look at the neural network as a whole and touch on some common terminologies associated with it. The chapter starts with an explanation of neural networks. Then, we move along to defining what exactly a perceptron is, with a brief introduction to it. Further, we will compare a single-layer neural network with a multilayer neural network, emphasizing the structure of the neural network.

In the subsequent section, we will look at the various activation functions available. Next, we will define bias and weight and describe why they are useful. In the next section, we will touch on a neural network example.

In the last section, we will look at how to traverse a neural network. We will cover backpropagation and touch on forward propagation and feedforward neural networks.

© Abhishek Nandy, Manisha Biswas 2018
A. Nandy and M. Biswas, *Neural Networks in Unity*,
https://doi.org/10.1007/978-1-4842-3673-4_1

Introducing Neural Networks

An artificial neural network is similar to a biological neural network in a brain. A biological neural network works as follows: *information flows in, is processed by the neurons, and the results flow out.*

The basis of the neuron is to react to previously learned patterns.

When we are creating the same kind of replication in terms of technology and computer science, we call it an **artificial neural network**.

Just like the biological neuron, information flows in, is processed by an artificial neural network, and results flow out (Figure 1-1).

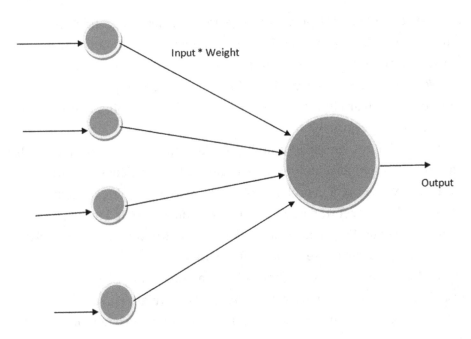

Figure 1-1. *A neural network*

The single process becomes a mathematical formula that is the combination of summation + threshold.

In terms of mathematics, it will be similar to a polynomial:

(In1 * weight1) + (In2 * Weight2) + (In3 * Weight3) = Summation.

Digging Deeper into Neural Networks

Let us discuss more about neural networks.

Neural networks consist of:

- Input

- Output

- Weights and biases

- Activation function

Artificial neural networks are generally a chain of nodes associated with each other via the link from which they start interacting accordingly.

Neurons perform operations and carry that result.

Let us consider a scenario. Suppose that a new movie has been released at a movie theater. Now there are nearby options to watch this movie in a particular movie theater. Our brain makes a split second decision where we are going to watch the movie.

The split second decision is pretty obvious for the brain to trigger from the neurons we have, but for same kinds of replication in a computer it is tough. For that, we have devised a mathematical approach. Let's take an example.

We have a single neuron whose threshold value is 7. We need to find out if the neuron will trigger or not (Figure 1-2).

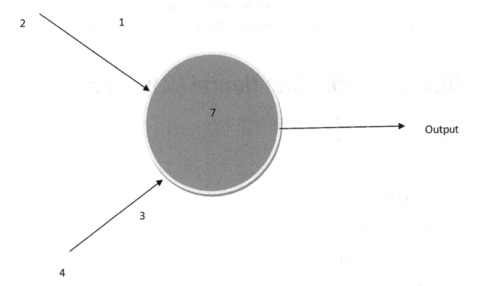

Figure 1-2. *Formulating the mathematical formula*

Now let us see how an artificial neuron does the mathematical calculation.

The criterion is that when the threshold 7 is reached, the neuron will trigger.

The summation rule says, as shown in Figure 1-2, if one input point has value 2 and weight 1 and the other has input value 4 and weight 3, then

$\sum$ Summation $= (2 * 1) + (4 * 3) = 2 + 12 = 14.$

As 14 is greater then 7, the neuron will trigger. This is the way a neuron works.

Perceptron

In neural network implementation, a perceptron is very significant. When a neural network consists of a single layer, we call it a **perceptron**. It is used mostly in supervised learning to classify the data.

A perceptron is composed of four different things:

- Input values or one input layer

- Weights and bias

- Summation

- Activation function

When we look at a perceptron, it looks as shown in Figure 1-3.

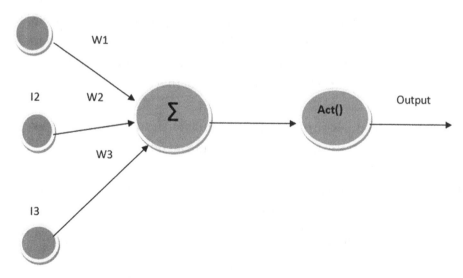

Figure 1-3. *Activation function*

It is generally used as a binary classifier. When we are looking to classify data into two parts, we rely on a perceptron.

Activation Function and Its Different Types

In this section, we will touch upon one of the most important topics in terms of neural network, known as **activation function**.

The activation looks like Figure 1-4.

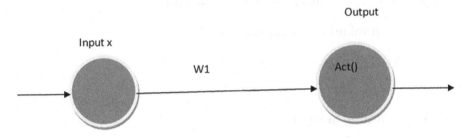

Figure 1-4. *One input activation function*

An activation function allows nonlinear properties to be constructed. The activation function is used to predict the output of a neural network, that is, yes or no. It maps the resulting values in the range of 0 to 1 or −1 to 1, etc. (depending upon the function). It plays a mjor role in an artificial neural network because it generates an output that becomes an input for the next layer in the stack.

The general purpose of an activation function is to convert the input into an artificial neural network and then into an output.

Activation functions are of various types, and we will discuss them here. There are many activation functions used in machine learning, of which the most commonly used are listed below.

- Identity function

- Binary step

- Logistic or sigmoid

- Tanh

- Arctan

- Rectified linear unit(ReLU)

- Leaky ReLU

- Softmax

Identity Function

In this function, we have x as an input, it will give us x itself (Figure 1-5).

$F(x) = x$

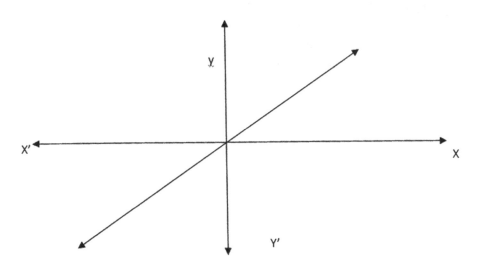

Figure 1-5. *The identity function*

Binary Step Function

This function is very important in classifiers. If we want to classify between 1 and 0, it is very useful.

- If our input is greater then 0, it gives us value 1.

- If our input is less then 0, it gives value 0.

$F(x) = 0$ for $x < 0$
1 for $x >= 0$

Logistic or Sigmoid

Whatever the input, the sigmoid function maps it between 0 and 1 (Figure 1-6). It is very useful in neural networks.

$Sig(x) = 1/1 + e^{-x}$

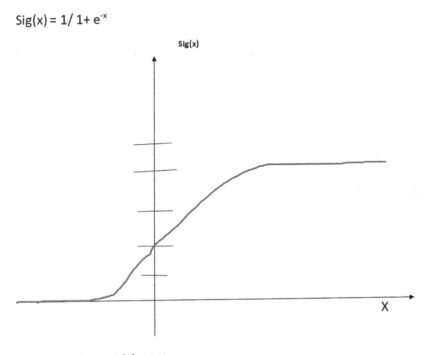

Figure 1-6. Sigmoid function curve

Tan H Function

Useful for neural networks (Figure 1-7).

$F(x) = \tan h(x) = (2/1 + e{-2}x) - 1$

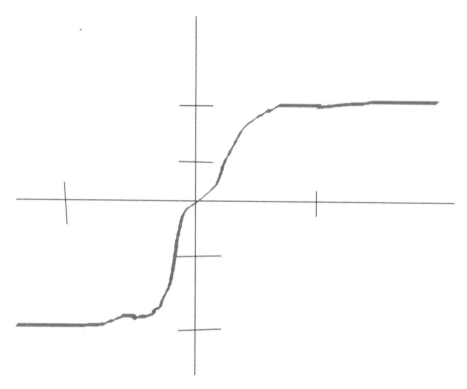

Figure 1-7. *Tan H function curve*

Arctan Function

Whatever the input, the arctan function maps it between $-\pi/2$ and $+\pi/2$ (Figure 1-8).

$$F(x) = \tan{-1}(x)$$

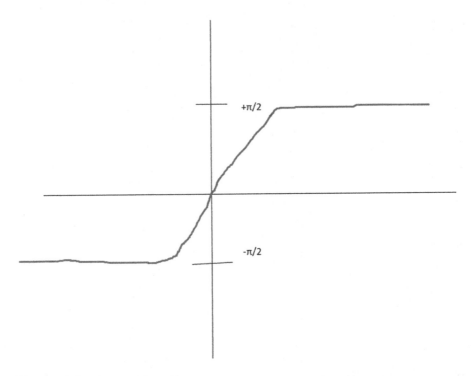

Figure 1-8. *Arctan function*

Rectified Linear Unit

ReLU returns 0 if it receives negative input and returns the input value back if it is positive (Figure 1-9).

$F(x) = 0$ for $x < 0$

x for $x >= 0$

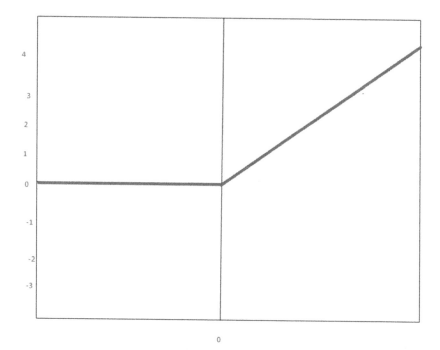

Figure 1-9. *ReLU function*

11

Leaky ReLU

Leaky ReLU is very popular for deep learning. It removes the negative part of the function (Figure 1-10).

$F(x) = 0.01x$ for $x < 0$

x for $x >= 0$

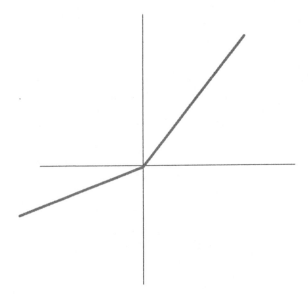

Figure 1-10. *Leaky ReLU curve*

It doesn't make the negative input 0, however; it just reduces the magnitude of it.

Softmax Function

The softmax function is used to import probabilities when we have more than one output.

It is useful for finding the most probable occurrence of an output with respect to other outputs.

This is used for imparting probabilities.

$$\sigma(z)_j = \frac{e^{z_j}}{\sum_{k=1}^{K} e^{z_k}} \text{ for } j = 1, \ldots, K.$$

Biases and Weights

These are important factors when we are dealing with neural networks.

When we create a neural network, we need some additional factors to stabilize the nework. Hence, bias and weights come into the picture. The essential understanding of bias is that when we are applying an activation function to an input, bias allows us to shift the values either left or right.

Let's create a simple neural network (Figure 1-11).

Figure 1-11. *A simple neural network*

Now we consider there is no bias in this network. The output of the network is the basis of two things, per the summation rule (Figure 1-12), that is, $\sum Wi * Xi$
where Wi is the weight and Xi is the input. We have single weight and single input, so, the resultant is the multiplication.

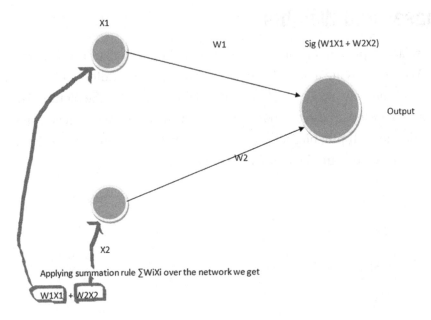

Figure 1-12. *Summation rule*

For a single unit network, the output as we know is found by multiplying with input $X0$ and then passing it over to the activation function. If we apply different weight values, the curve changes accordingly (Figure 1-13).

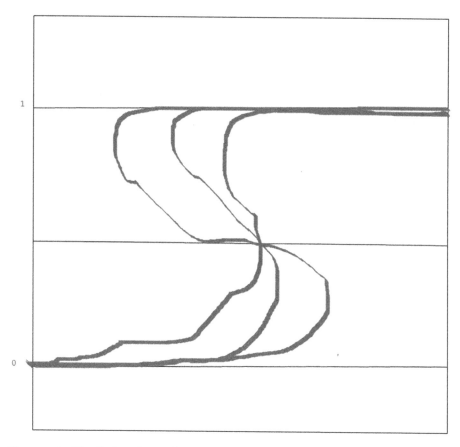

Figure 1-13. *Role of weights*

Using weights, we only change the steepness of the curve but cannot shift the values either right or left.

For shifting the values either left or right we need bias (Figure 1-14).

Input

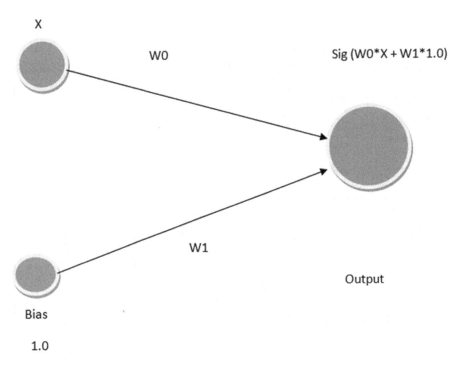

Figure 1-14. *Applying bias*

Bias is useful if we want a network to output the value of 0 when x has a value of, say, 1 (Figure 1-15).

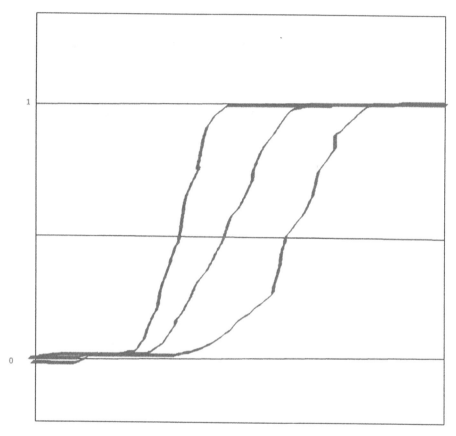

Figure 1-15. *Role of bias*

Neural Network from Scratch

Neural networks have become popular with the advent of faster computers and tons of data.

Building a model is the basis for doing lots of analysis. When we build a model, we create a concrete structure for applying machine learning to it.

When the model is being created, we train it using the input and output data to make it better at implying pattern recognition for best results.

We will build a model with a three-layer neural network–the programmable approach as taken by the Python language (Figure 1-16).

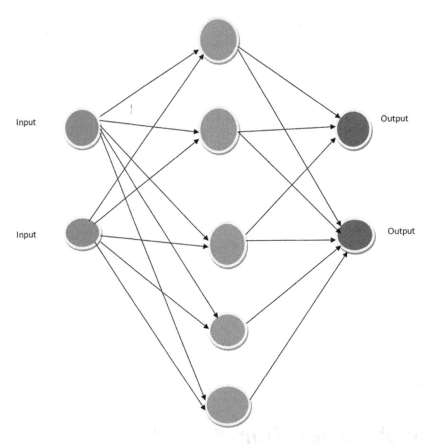

Figure 1-16. *The neural network we will be creating now*

Before getting into the programming mold, we will go through the steps we are to perform.

1. Train a neural network on input and output data.

2. Use Python as the basis of programming.

3. Import libraries, one of them being NumPy.

4. Create a neural network model now.

5. Create and utilize an activation function.

6. Initialize input data.

7. Create an output dataset.

8. Generate a random number.

9. Create synapse matrices.

10. Create the training code (training step).

11. In the next step, update weight.

Let's start now.

We will be using NumPy. NumPy is a library specially meant for scientific computing using Python. When we are considering NumPy, it generally consists of a powerful n-dimensional array that is multidimensional and contains items of the same type and size.

We have advanced functions to utilize. Within NumPy, we have support for applying linear algebra, Fourier transform, and useful random number capabilities.

First we will import NumPy.

```
import NumPy as np
```

Next we will be creating a function that maps to a value between 0 and 1. The function that we would be using is called the sigmoid function.

The function that we create will be run on every neuron in our network when it attracts a dataset.

It's useful for creating probabilities.

```
def nonlin(x,deriv=False):
    if(deriv==True):
        return x*(1-x)
    return 1/(1+np.exp(-x))
```

Once we have created that, we will initialize the input dataset as a matrix. Each row is a different training example. Each column represents a different neuron.

Now we have four training examples and three input neurons each.

```
X = np.array([[0,0,1],[0,1,1],[1,0,1],[1,1,1]])
```

Then we will create our output dataset.

```
Y = np.array([[0],[1],[1],[0]])
```

This contains four examples and one output neuron each. As we will be generating a random number, we seed them to make it deterministic.

```
np.random.seed(1)
```

Random numbers are generated with the same seed so that we get the same set of generated numbers (starting point) every time we run our program. This is useful for debugging.

Next, we will work with **Synapses**.

Synapses are linked from one neuron to another. It is a connection between each neuron in one layer to every neuron in a subsequent layer.

Since we have three layers in the neuron we need two synapse matrices.

Each synapse has a random weight associated with it.

```
syn0 = 2*np.random.random((3,4)) - 1
syn1 = 2*np.random.random((4,1)) - 1
```

Now, we will run the training module. We will create a for loop that iterates the network for a given dataset.

We will start off by creating the first layer matrix multiplication between each layer and its synapse, then we will run sigmoid on all the values in the matrix to create the next layer.

```
l0 = X
    l1 = nonlin(np.dot(l0,syn0))
    l2 = nonlin(np.dot(l1, syn1))
```

Let us compare the expected value using subtraction to get the error rate.

```
l2_error = Y - l2
    if(iter % 10000) == 0:    # Only print the error every 10000
    steps, to save time and limit the amount of output.
        print("Error: " + str(np.mean(np.abs(l2_error))))
```

Let us recapitulate what we have done.

L is the input data.

Now comes the predicting state. We perform matrix multiplication.

The next layer contains the output of the predicting data.

The subsequent layer is more of a refined prediction.

We will also print the error rate to check it goes down over a period of time.

Taking it further, we apply the following changes to the neural network.

Now we multiply the error rate with the result of our sigmoid function. The function will allow us to get the derivate of output prediction from layer 2; this will give us delta, from which we find the error rate of our prediction when we update our synapses on each iteration.

```
l2_delta = l2_error*nonlin(l2, deriv=True)
```

Then we will see how much layer 1 contributed to the error in layer 2; this is called **backpropagation**. We will get this by multiplying the l2_delta with Synapses 1's transpose.

```
l1_error = l2_delta.dot(syn1.T)
```

Then we get l1 delta by multiplying its error with (l1_error) with the result of the sigmoid function. The function is used to find the derivatives of layer 1.

Now that we have deltas of all layers, we can use them to update the synapse weights to reduce the error rate more and more on each iteration. This is an algorithm called **gradient descent**. To do this, we will multiply each layer by its delta.

The following is the full code.

```
import NumPy as np

# sigmoid function
def nonlin(x,deriv=False):
    if(deriv==True):
        return x*(1-x)
    return 1/(1+np.exp(-x))

# input dataset
X = np.array([[0,0,1],[0,1,1],[1,0,1],[1,1,1]])

# output dataset
Y = np.array([[0],[1],[1],[0]])

# seed random numbers to make calculation
# deterministic (just a good practice)
np.random.seed(1)

# initialize weights randomly with mean 0
syn0 = 2*np.random.random((3,4)) - 1
syn1 = 2*np.random.random((4,1)) - 1
```

```python
for iter in range(60000):

    # forward propagation
    l0 = X
    l1 = nonlin(np.dot(l0,syn0))
    l2 = nonlin(np.dot(l1, syn1))

    # Backpropagation of errors using the chain rule.
    l2_error = Y - l2
    if(iter % 10000) == 0:    # Only print the error every 10000
    steps, to save time and limit the amount of output.
        print("Error L2: " + str(np.mean(np.abs(l2_error))))

    # how much did we miss?
    # l1_error = l2_delta.dot(syn1.T)

    # multiply how much we missed by the
    # slope of the sigmoid at the values in l1
    l2_delta = l2_error*nonlin(l2, deriv=True)

    l1_error = l2_delta.dot(syn1.T)

    l1_delta = l1_error * nonlin(l1,deriv=True)
    if(iter % 10000) == 0:    # Only print the error every 10000
    steps, to save time and limit the amount of output.
        print("Error L1: " + str(np.mean(np.abs(l1_error))))

    # update weights
    syn1 += l1.T.dot(l2_delta)
    syn0 += l0.T.dot(l1_delta)
```

```
print ("Output After Training for l1:")
print (l1)
print ("Output After training for l2")
print(l2)
```

The output looks like Figure 1-17.

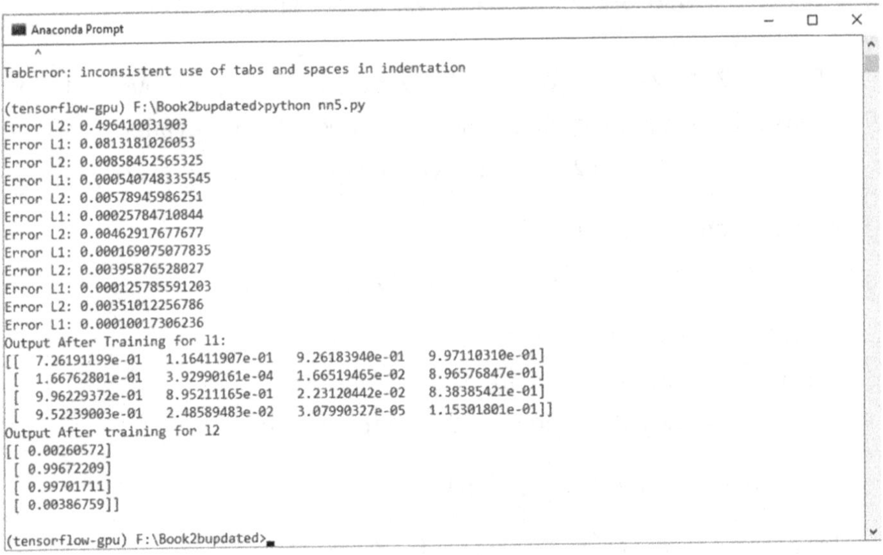

Figure 1-17. *Output of the neural network*

We may get an error while running the code, such as TabError: inconsistent use of tabs and spaces in indentation (Figure 1-18).

```
(tensorflow-gpu) F:\Book2bupdated>python nn5.py
  File "nn5.py", line 34
    print("Error L1: " + str(np.mean(np.abs(l1_error))))
                                                      ^
TabError: inconsistent use of tabs and spaces in indentation
```

Figure 1-18. *Error for tabs and spaces*

It can be rectified in the following way. In any IDE (integrated development environment) that you are using, change the blank operation from tab to space (Figure 1-19).

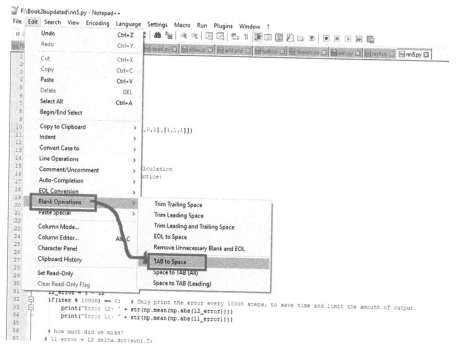

Figure 1-19. *Rectifying the error*

Backpropagation

Backpropagation is a methodical approach especially famous in deep learning, where we calculate the gradient in order to find errors and match the weights found in the neural network.

Backpropagation leads to differantiation propagating back to the network starting point. It uses the differentiation chain rule to propagate back.

Summary

In this chapter, we have gone through the basics of a neural network and how the neural network has evolved. We touched upon activation function and its types.

In the next chapter, we will start using neural networks in Unity, as well as implementing machine learning agents to it.

CHAPTER 2

Unity ML-Agents

In this chapter, we will study how Unity ML-Agents work. First, we will start with a brief description of Unity IDE and then we will look at this feature from Unity. We will check on some demos and then create one simulation of our own. We will see how the agents are trained using Python.

Unity IDE

Unity IDE is a game engine that supports developing games, with a physics engine already available to build the games too. It supports multiple formats including Windows, Linux, MacOS, and other devices too. The Unity ML-Agents that they have declared is a very good extension, so we can rapidly prototype lots of simulations based on Unity for research purposes.

Getting Started with Machine Learning Agents

There are so many changes happening with Unity. They came up with an exciting feature (using the ML-Agents) that helps developers to train the game they created using ML implementation, so that the entire process can be replicated by the trained model and we can compare the differences. This method uses the reinforcment learning approach.

© Abhishek Nandy, Manisha Biswas 2018
A. Nandy and M. Biswas, *Neural Networks in Unity*,
https://doi.org/10.1007/978-1-4842-3673-4_2

Reinforcement learning is that part of machine learning where the basis of learning is based upon environments and simulations, where software agents (software program) take actions with effect from environment so that we can provide a reward.

The steps we need to perform for the machine learning agents to work perfectly are:

1. First we have to see that Unity IDE is installed. Download and install the Unity game engine from the following link.

   ```
   https://store.unity.com/download?ref=personal
   ```

2. We have to clone the machine learning GitHub repo.

   The following link will take us to the machine learning background (Figure 2-1).

The Unity ML-Agents contain the latest version, so no need to search for a specific version.

```
https://github.com/Unity-Technologies/ml-agents
```

Figure 2-1. *The Unity ML-Agents website link*

3. When we click Download ML-Agents, it will take us to the GitHub repo.

It takes us to the following link, where we have the important files for our machine learning agent unity.

```
https://github.com/Unity-Technologies/ml-agents
```

4. The web page looks like Figure 2-2.

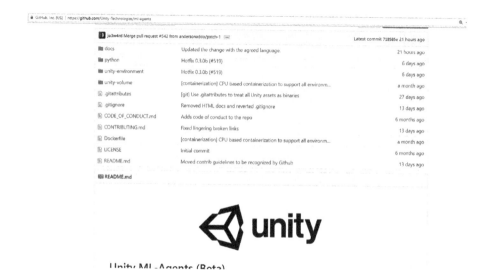

Figure 2-2. *GitHub repo to be cloned*

The essential files for the project are there in the repo, so we can get started with it.

Let's Start with TensorFlow

Tensorflow is a framework that is primarily meant for dataflow-based work. It uses Ttensors and their approach to nodes in a very effective way, so that we can easily implement it in machine learning as well with deep learning.

It has very good documentation from the Google side, so we can learn it easily.

TensorFlow information and downloads are available in the following link.

```
https://www.tensorflow.org/
```

Understanding Anaconda

We need to discuss Anaconda too. Anaconda is a machine learning library distribution for Python that contains lots of important libraries for machine learning and deep learning.

Anaconda distribution is available from the following link.

```
https://www.anaconda.com/download/
```

First, we install Anaconda distribution for Python. After that we will see that the Anaconda prompt is available. We need to open the prompt (it is similar to a command prompt).

When we start, we need to create an environment. The command to create a new environment is shown below.

```
conda create --name myenv
```

myenv is the environment name, which you can update or change according to your liking.

If we want to create an environment with a specific version of Python, we need to use the following process.

```
conda create -n myenv python=3.4
```

To activete an environment we created, we need to use the following command.

```
Activate <envname>
```

If we want to get out of the environment, we will use

```
Deactivate
```

If we want to add an environment with a GPU version of TensorFlow, we will have to do the following. For a GPU version of TensorFlow we need to have a graphics card installed to work properly.

The steps are:

1. Download and Install CUDA.

CUDA has different versions. We need CUDA Version 8.0. I have 8.0, 9.0, and 9.1 installed and set up identically to this guide for each version. Stick with 8.0 for now to get that working. I set up the other versions to prepare for the possiblity of TensorFlow GPU supporting other CUDA versions.

---

2. Go to CUDA Toolkit downloads.

3. Scroll down to Legacy Releases or here.

4. Click the version you want from CUDA Toolkit X.Y: for 8.0, we'll see CUDA Toolkit 8.0 GA, so replace *<Z>* with the highest number available. I downloaded CUDA Toolkit 8.0 GA2.

   For 9.0, the file is CUDA Toolkit 9.0; for 9.1, the file is CUDA Toolkit 9.1.

5. Select your operating system; mine is
   OS: Windows
   Architecture: x86_64
   Version: 10

6. After CUDA downloads, run the file downloaded and install with Express settings. This might take a while and flicker the screen (due to it being for the graphics card).

7. Verify you now have the following path on your system.
   `C:\Program Files\NVIDIA GPU Computing Toolkit\CUDA\v8.0`

8. Download and install cuDNN.

   For this, you'll need an NVIDIA developer account. It's free.

9. Create a free NVIDIA Developer membership here.

10. After you sign up, go to `https://developer. nvidia.com/cudnn`.

11. Click Download (ignore the current listed version for now).

12. Agree to the terms.

13. Remember how previously we needed cuDNN v6.0? You might see this listed here, or you might not. If you don't, just select Archived cuDNN Releases.

14. Click the version you need, as well as the system you need. I clicked:

15. Download cuDNN v6.0 (April 27, 2017) for CUDA 8.0,

    then cuDNN v6.0 Library for Windows 10.

16. Go to your recent downloaded zip file, something like `C:\Users\teamcfe\Downloads\cudnn-8.0-windows10-x64-v6.0.zip`

17. Unzip the file.

18. Open Cuda; you should see:
    bin/
    include/
    lib/

19. Copy and paste the three folders in `C:\Users\j\Downloads\cudnn-8.0-windows10-x64-v6.0.zip\cuda` to `C:\Program Files\NVIDIA GPU Computing Toolkit\CUDA\v8.0`

Do note that dragging and dropping will merge the folders and not replace them; I don't believe the same is true for Mac/Linux. If it asks you to replace anything, say no and just drag and drop each folder's contents from cuDNN to Cuda. It might ask about admin privileges, for which you should just say yes.

---

20. Verify if you did the last step correctly; you should be able to find this path.
`C:\Program Files\NVIDIA GPU Computing Toolkit\CUDA\v8.0\lib\x64\cudnn.lib`

21. Update the %PATH% on the system.

    Update your system environment variables' PATH to have

    `C:\Program Files\NVIDIA GPU Computing Toolkit\CUDA\v8.0\bin`
    `C:\Program Files\NVIDIA GPU Computing Toolkit\CUDA\v8.0\libnvvp`

    To get here, do a start menu/cortana search to Edit the system environment variables.

    It should open System Properties and the Advanced tab.

    Click Environment Variables.

    Under System Variables, look for PATH, and click Edit. Add the two lines from step 21.

Now we will download the ml agents file. If you are not conversant with git, you can directly download the file as a zip file and then extract it.

What Is the NVDIA CUDA Toolkit?

The NVIDIA CUDA Toolkit is used for creating high-performance GPU-accelerated applications. The Toolkit includes GPU-accelerated libraries, debugging and optimization tools, and a C/C++ complier and a runtime library to deploy our application. It's an industry benchmark for deep learning for the entire training process to work seamlessly. We use the underlying principles of CUDA for better performance of TensorFlow GPU.

GPU-Accelerated TensorFlow

Training in deep learning takes lots of time. As we implement the GPU version of TensorFlow, the speed of training increases by 50%.

Now, with the GPU version, you can train the models in hours instead of days. Using the GPU version hence makes training the machine learning process much faster and gets more accurate results. Let's clone the repo using the GPU version of TensorFlow.

We will be using Anaconda and first we will have to activate the environment.

```
(C:\Users\abhis\Anaconda3) C:\Users\abhis>activate tensorflow-gpu
```

After activating it will enable the environment.

```
(tensorflow-gpu) C:\Users\abhis>
```

Now we will clone the repo (Figure 2-3). Let us assume we do it in Desktop.

```
(tensorflow-gpu) C:\Users\abhis\Desktop>git clone
https://github.com/Unity-Technologies/ml-agents.git
```

If we are not familiar with git, we can directly download and save the file as a zip file, unzip it in a folder, and start working with it.

```
(tensorflow-gpu) C:\Users\abhis\Desktop>
(tensorflow-gpu) C:\Users\abhis\Desktop>git clone https://github.com/Unity-Technologies/ml-agents.git
Cloning into 'ml-agents'...
remote: Counting objects: 8868, done.
remote: Compressing objects: 100% (48/48), done.
remote: Total 8868 (delta 24), reused 7 (delta 0), pack-reused 8820
Receiving objects: 100% (8868/8868), 151.49 MiB | 139.00 KiB/s, done.
Resolving deltas: 100% (5444/5444), done.

(tensorflow-gpu) C:\Users\abhis\Desktop>
```

Figure 2-3. *Cloning the GitHub repo*

1. Let's open up Unity.

    When you open Unity, it looks as shown in Figure 2-4.

Figure 2-4. *Opening the project file in Unity IDE*

2. Now we will have to open the cloned project. At the
    top right-hand side we have an option called Open;
    we need to click that.

    We have to get inside the repo, then select
    unity-environment as the folder (Figure 2-5).

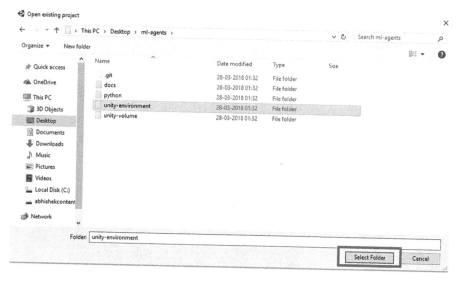

Figure 2-5. *Selecting the appropriate folder*

After selecting unity-environment, the game engine
will open up.

3. We need to accept the details if we are using an
    older version of Unity (Figure 2-6).

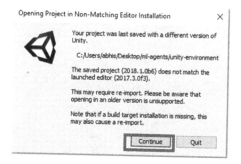

Figure 2-6. *We accept to continue*

4. When everything is done, the Unity IDE will open up
    (Figure 2-7).

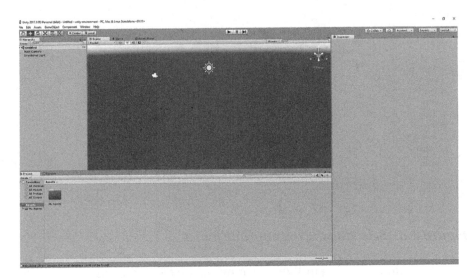

Figure 2-7. *The Unity IDE*

Let us go through the file structure of the GitHub ML-Agents repo
(Figure 2-8).

UnityRI2 > ml-agents-master >

Name	Date modified	Type	Size
docs	01-11-2017 08:38	File folder	
images	01-11-2017 08:38	File folder	
python	28-03-2018 03:43	File folder	
unity-environment	28-03-2018 17:57	File folder	
	01-11-2017 08:38	Text Document	2 KB
CODE_OF_CONDUCT	01-11-2017 08:38	MD File	4 KB
LICENSE	01-11-2017 08:38	File	12 KB
README	01-11-2017 08:38	MD File	2 KB

(F:

Figure 2-8. *The ml-agents folder*

The important files in the hierarchy are the Python folder and the unity-environment.

Within the Unity environment we have the Assets folder, which contains all the objects required to run the scene as well as the C# scripts for enabling the movements of the object.

Within the Python folder we have the script for training the exe file generated after compiling the project.

The unity environment contains the following important Unity Assets file (Figure 2-9).

Name	Date modified	Type	Size
Assets	21-02-2018 18:43	File folder	
Library	28-03-2018 17:57	File folder	
ProjectSettings	28-03-2018 13:00	File folder	
UnityPackageManager	07-11-2017 01:09	File folder	
README	01-11-2017 08:38	MD File	4 KB

> UnityRI2 > ml-agents-master > unity-environment >

Figure 2-9. *The unity environments folder*

The Python folder is important, as we have to keep the build files in this folder.

We need to save the file in the Python subfolder, because the necessary file for traing the exe we generated is residing in this folder. The code for training is also present there.

Building a Project in Unity

Let's now start with the project.

1. We open up Unity, if it was not already done (Figure 2-10).

Figure 2-10. *Unity engine opening up*

2. We have to open up the cloned project.

    We refer to the same project over here from the Unity ML-Agents file we downloaded from the website. We need to open it up in Unity for compiling and also changing the details of the project.

There are a lot of examples in the repo; we will start
with 3D Ball (Figure 2-11).

Figure 2-11. *The example we will be working on*

3. We will open the Scene file (Figure 2-12).

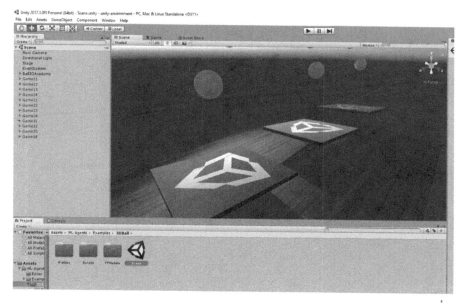

Figure 2-12. *The scene file*

4. The changes that are to be made can be found in the Hierarchy tab, the most important one being Ball3DAcademy (Figure 2-13).

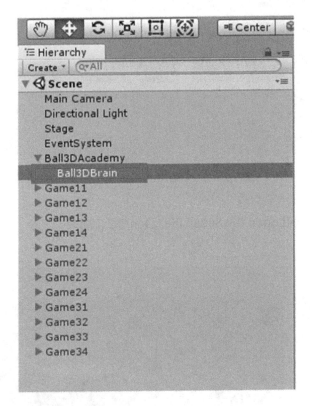

Figure 2-13. *The Ball3dBrain*

5. To try out how the simulation works with a player
    setting, we have to go inside the inspector window.

    We will have to change the brain type to player
    (Figure 2-14).

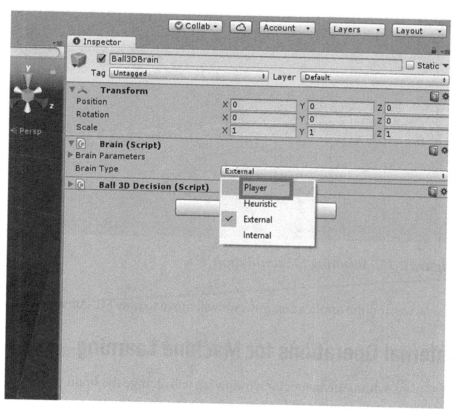

Figure 2-14. *Changing the player type to external*

6. If we run the application now, we will be able to see how it works within player mode without the ML-Agents being added (Figure 2-15).

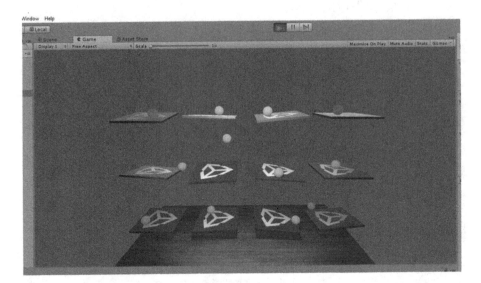

Figure 2-15. *Running the simulation*

As we stop the application now, we will move to how ML-Agents work.

Internal Operations for Machine Learning

First of all, within the inspector window we will change the brain type to external.

We have to make some changes within the edit tab of the Unity IDE.

1. We will go inside edit ➤ project settings ➤ player as shown in Figure 2-16).

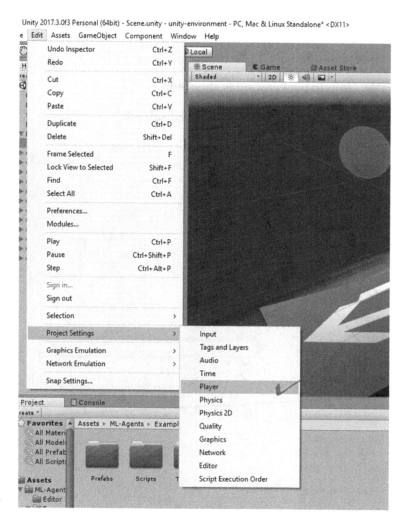

Figure 2-16. *Getting inside the player options*

2. Within the inspector window (Figure 2-17), we
    will have to check that in the tab resolution and
    presentation

    • Run in background is checked.

    • Display Resolution Dialog is disabled.

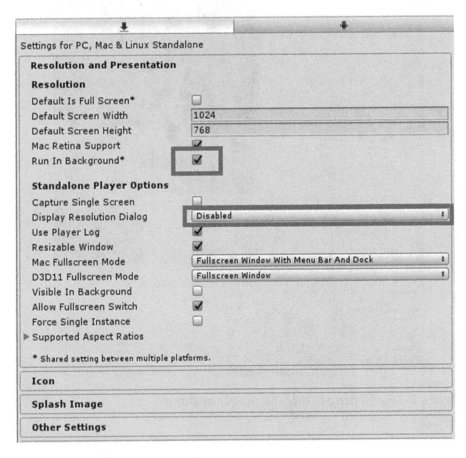

Figure 2-17. *Inspector window*

3. We will go inside the file and save the scene.

4. Again we will go back to the file tab and inside the
    Build Settings (Figure 2-18).

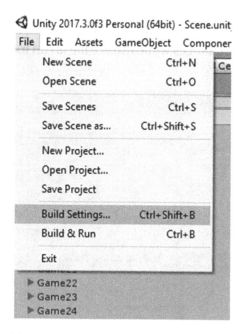

Figure 2-18. *Building the exe file*

5.   We will have to add the scene and select it and then
     click Build (Figure 2-19).

     We need to check the options for Development
     Build, so we can track any error while running the
     project exe. With development build enabled, we
     can see the changes while the exe file is run too.

Figure 2-19. *Selecting the scene and building it*

6. When we click Build, it will ask us to save the file
   (Figure 2-20). We name the file too.

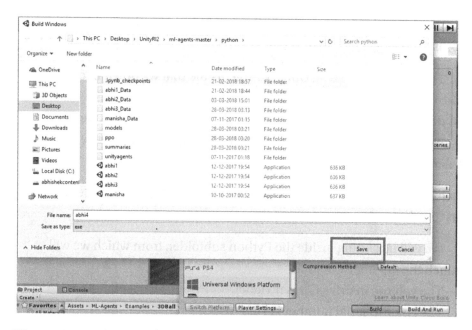

Figure 2-20. *Saving the exe file*

7. We will save the file in Python sub directory of the
   project.

Training Anaconda in Python Mode

Now we will have to start Anaconda, as we will be training it in Python
mode.

We will activate the environment.

First of all we will have to open the command prompt; as the
command prompt comes up we need to activate the Anaconda
environment we created for tensorflow-gpu.

We have to write the following command.

```
Activate tensorflow-gpu
```

```
(C:\Users\abhis\Anaconda3) C:\Users\abhis>activate tensorflow-gpu
(tensorflow-gpu) C:\Users\abhis>
```

First of all, there is the Unity Ml-Agents file that we download or have added as a git. We need to get inside the file, which contains the Python subdirectory, as within that we have built the Unity game exe file.

Now we will go to the place where the file is cloned and the exe file is generated.

```
(tensorflow-gpu) C:\Users\abhis\Desktop\UnityR12\ml-agents-
master>dir
```

We will be getting inside the Python subfolder, from which we will launch the Jupyter Notebook.

The volume in drive C has no label.

The volume serial number is 1E9F-654C.

```
Directory of C:\Users\abhis\Desktop\UnityR12\ml-agents-master

01-11-2017  08:38    <DIR>             .
01-11-2017  08:38    <DIR>             ..
01-11-2017  08:38               1,108 .gitignore
01-11-2017  08:38               3,191 CODE_OF_CONDUCT.md
01-11-2017  08:38    <DIR>             docs
01-11-2017  08:38    <DIR>             images
01-11-2017  08:38              11,348 LICENSE
29-03-2018  00:16    <DIR>             python
01-11-2017  08:38               1,490 README.md
28-03-2018  21:48    <DIR>             unity-environment
               4 File(s)         17,137 bytes
               6 Dir(s)  29,652,058,112 bytes free
```

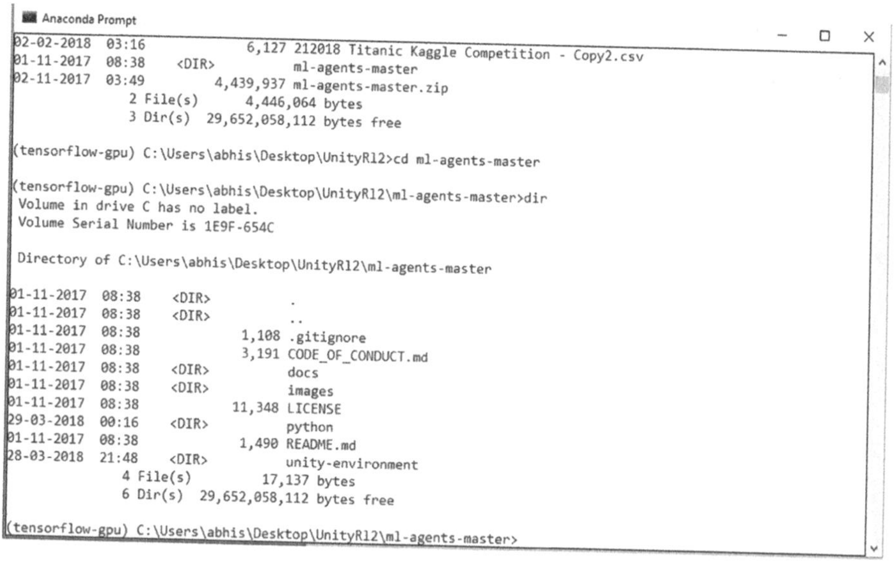

Figure 2-21. *Analyzing the ml-agents-master file*

We will get inside the Python folder.

We will have to start Jupyter Notebook.

Working with Jupyter Notebook

What is Jupyter Notebook?

Jupyter Notebook is a client server-based application that allows us write Python notebook online in a web browser mode.

To enable Jupyter Notebook, we have to put in this command.

```
(tensorflow-gpu) C:\Users\abhis\Desktop\UnityR12\ml-agents-master\python>jupyter notebook
```

It opens up in a web browser and appropriate files are shown. It is shown in Figure 2-22.

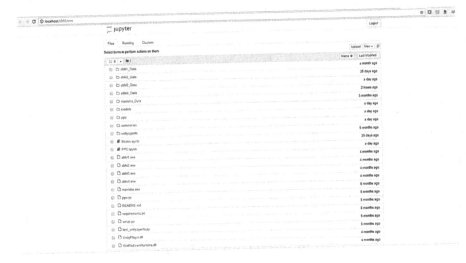

Figure 2-22.   *Opening Jupyter Notebook*

The two important files needed by us are shown in Figure 2-23.

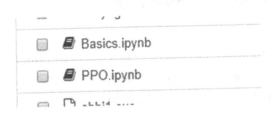

Figure 2-23.   *The important IPython files*

We will open the Basics.ipynb first.

We will go through the basics of Jupyter notebook.

First we have to load the dependencies.

The necessary files are all structured in the Jupyter Notebook that comes bundled up with the ML-Agents we downloaded.

If some of the libraries such as NumPy and matplotlib are not installed, we have to install them from Anaconda.

```
conda install -c anaconda numpy
```

For matplotlib we use the following command.

```
conda install -c conda-forge matplotlib
```

We will import the necessary files to train our ML-Agents.

```
import matplotlib.pyplot as plt
import numpy as np

from unityagents import UnityEnvironment

%matplotlib inline
```

After that we will have to name the exe file that we created in Unity, so that we can train the model. We will run the environment in training mode.

```
env_name = "abhi4" # Name of the Unity environment binary to
launch
train_mode = True # Whether to run the environment in training
or inference mode
```

Now we will start the environment, so that communication between the Und the environity anment created starts.

In the Unity script, we have a brain that controls the agents and is responsible for what the agents will do.

```
env = UnityEnvironment(file_name=env_name)

# Examine environment parameters
print(str(env))
```

```
# Set the default brain to work with
default_brain = env.brain_names[0]
brain = env.brains[default_brain]
```

In the next section we will observe the states they are in currently.

```
# Reset the environment
env_info = env.reset(train_mode=train_mode)[default_brain]
```

```
# Examine the state space for the default brain
print("Agent state looks like: \n{}".format(env_info.
states[0]))
```

```
# Examine the observation space for the default brain
for observation in env_info.observations:
    print("Agent observations look like:")
    if observation.shape[3] == 3:
        plt.imshow(observation[0,:,:,:])
    else:
        plt.imshow(observation[0,:,:,0])
```

In the next section we will choose actions based on the action_space_ type of our default brain.

```
for episode in range(10):
    env_info = env.reset(train_mode=train_mode)[default_brain]
    done = False
    episode_rewards = 0
    while not done:
        if brain.action_space_type == 'continuous':
            env_info = env.step(np.random.randn(len
            (env_info.agents),

                                    brain.action_
                                    space_size))
                                    [default_brain]
```

```
else:
    env_info = env.step(np.random.randint(0, brain.
    action_space_size,

                                      size=(len(env_
                                      info.agents))))
                                      [default_
                                      brain]

    episode_rewards += env_info.rewards[0]
    done = env_info.local_done[0]
print("Total reward this episode: {}".format
(episode_rewards))
```

After that we close the environment.

```
env.close()
```

When we start the environment, it will launch the exe. We need to click Allow (Figure 2-24).

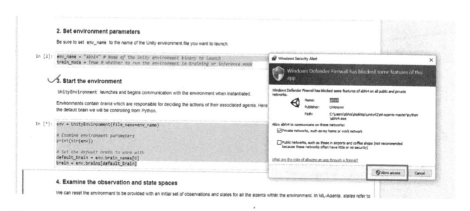

Figure 2-24. *Allowing access to the Unity file*

The agents will start as shown in Figure 2-25.

```
In [3]: env = UnityEnvironment(file_name=env_name)

        # Examine environment parameters
        print(str(env))

        # Set the default brain to work with
        default_brain = env.brain_names[0]
        brain = env.brains[default_brain]

        INFO:unityagents.environment:
        'Ball3DAcademy' started successfully!

        Unity Academy name: Ball3DAcademy
                Number of brains: 1
                Reset Parameters :

        Unity brain name: Ball3DBrain
                Number of observations (per agent): 0
                State space type: continuous
                State space size (per agent): 8
                Action space type: continuous
                Action space size (per agent): 2
                Memory space size (per agent): 0
                Action descriptions: ,
```

Figure 2-25.   *The variables and parameters*

After that we see the reward (Figure 2-26).

5. Take random actions in the environment

Once we restart an environment, we can step the environment forward and provide actions to all of the agents within the environment. Here we simply choose random actions based on the `action_space_type` of the default brain.

```
In [6]: for episode in range(10):
            env_info = env.reset(train_mode=train_mode)[default_brain]
            done = False
            episode_rewards = 0
            while not done:
                if brain.action_space_type == 'continuous':
                    env_info = env.step(np.random.randn(len(env_info.agents),
                                        brain.action_space_size))[default_brain]
                else:
                    env_info = env.step(np.random.randint(0, brain.action_space_size,
                                        size=(len(env_info.agents))))[default_brain]
                episode_rewards += env_info.rewards[0]
                done = env_info.local_done[0]
            print("Total reward this episode: {}".format(episode_rewards))

        Total reward this episode: 0.40000000000000013
        Total reward this episode: 1.2000000000000006
        Total reward this episode: 0.6000000000000003
        Total reward this episode: 0.7000000000000004
        Total reward this episode: 0.9000000000000006
        Total reward this episode: 1.8000000000000012
        Total reward this episode: 0.8000000000000005
        Total reward this episode: 0.6000000000000003
        Total reward this episode: 0.6000000000000003
        Total reward this episode: 0.6000000000000003
```

Figure 2-26.   *Getting to know the reward*

Then we close the environment.

Proximity Policy Optimization

The next job we do is using Jupyter Notebook to get the proximal policy optimization. **PPO** is a proximity technique specially meant for applying reinforcement learning methods. We will do the same.

First we import the important files. Here we need TensorFlow for training the agents.

import numpy as np

```
import os
import tensorflow as tf

from ppo.history import *
from ppo.models import *
from ppo.trainer import Trainer
from unityagents import *
```

Then we declare the hyperparameters.

General parameters

```
max_steps = 50000 # Set maximum number of steps to run
environment.
run_path = "ppo" # The sub-directory name for model and summary
statistics
load_model = False # Whether to load a saved model.
train_model = True # Whether to train the model.
summary_freq = 10000 # Frequency at which to save training
statistics.
save_freq = 50000 # Frequency at which to save model.
env_name = "abhi4" # Name of the training environment file.

### Algorithm-specific parameters for tuning
gamma = 0.99 # Reward discount rate.
lambd = 0.95 # Lambda parameter for GAE.
```

```
time_horizon = 2048 # How many steps to collect per agent
before adding to buffer.
beta = 1e-3 # Strength of entropy regularization
num_epoch = 5 # Number of gradient descent steps per batch of
experiences.
epsilon = 0.2 # Acceptable threshold around ratio of old and
new policy probabilities.
buffer_size = 5000 # How large the experience buffer should be
before gradient descent.
learning_rate = 3e-4 # Model learning rate.
hidden_units = 64 # Number of units in hidden layer.
batch_size = 512 # How many experiences per gradient descent
update step.
```

After that we load the environments.

```
env = UnityEnvironment(file_name=env_name)
print(str(env))
brain_name = env.brain_names[0]
```

Then we train the environment using the TensorFlow framework and create the model graph.

```
tf.reset_default_graph()

# Create the Tensorflow model graph
ppo_model = create_agent_model(env, lr=learning_rate,
                               h_size=hidden_units,
                               epsilon=epsilon,
                               beta=beta, max_step=max_steps)

is_continuous = (env.brains[brain_name].action_space_type ==
"continuous")
```

```python
use_observations = (env.brains[brain_name].number_observations > 0)
use_states = (env.brains[brain_name].state_space_size > 0)

model_path = './models/{}'.format(run_path)
summary_path = './summaries/{}'.format(run_path)

if not os.path.exists(model_path):
    os.makedirs(model_path)

if not os.path.exists(summary_path):
    os.makedirs(summary_path)

init = tf.global_variables_initializer()
saver = tf.train.Saver()

with tf.Session() as sess:
    # Instantiate model parameters
    if load_model:
        print('Loading Model...')
        ckpt = tf.train.get_checkpoint_state(model_path)
        saver.restore(sess, ckpt.model_checkpoint_path)
    else:
        sess.run(init)
    steps = sess.run(ppo_model.global_step)
    summary_writer = tf.summary.FileWriter(summary_path)
    info = env.reset(train_mode=train_model)[brain_name]
    trainer = Trainer(ppo_model, sess, info, is_continuous,
    use_observations, use_states)
    while steps <= max_steps:
        if env.global_done:
            info = env.reset(train_mode=train_model)[brain_name]
        # Decide and take an action
        new_info = trainer.take_action(info, env, brain_name)
        info = new_info
```

```
        trainer.process_experiences(info, time_horizon, gamma,
    `   lambd)
        if len(trainer.training_buffer['actions']) > buffer_
        size and train_model:
            # Perform gradient descent with experience buffer
            trainer.update_model(batch_size, num_epoch)
        if steps % summary_freq == 0 and steps != 0 and train_
        model:
            # Write training statistics to tensorboard.
            trainer.write_summary(summary_writer, steps)
        if steps % save_freq == 0 and steps != 0 and train_model:
            # Save Tensorflow model
            save_model(sess, model_path=model_path,
            steps=steps, saver=saver)
        steps += 1
        sess.run(ppo_model.increment_step)
    # Final save Tensorflow model
    if steps != 0 and train_model:
        save_model(sess, model_path=model_path, steps=steps,
        saver=saver)
env.close()
export_graph(model_path, env_name)
```

Now we will export the TensorFlow graph, and the bytes file that is being created is taken inside the Unity so that we can see the ML-Agents performing.

```
export_graph(model_path, env_name)
```

As it works toward creating the environment, the following things are created first, as shown in Figure 2-27.

```
Load the environment

In [3]:  env = UnityEnvironment(file_name=env_name)
         print(str(env))
         brain_name = env.brain_names[0]

         INFO:unityagents.environment:
         'Ball3DAcademy' started successfully!

         Unity Academy name: Ball3DAcademy
                 Number of brains: 1
                 Reset Parameters :

         Unity brain name: Ball3DBrain
                 Number of observations (per agent): 0
                 State space type: continuous
                 State space size (per agent): 8
                 Action space type: continuous
                 Action space size (per agent): 2
                 Memory space size (per agent): 0
                 Action descriptions: ,
```

Figure 2-27. *The features are created*

After that we start training the model (Figure 2-28).

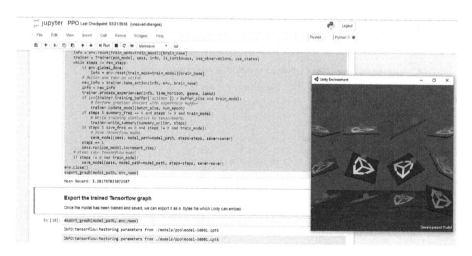

Figure 2-28. *Training has started*

Then we export the TensorFlow graph (Figure 2-29).

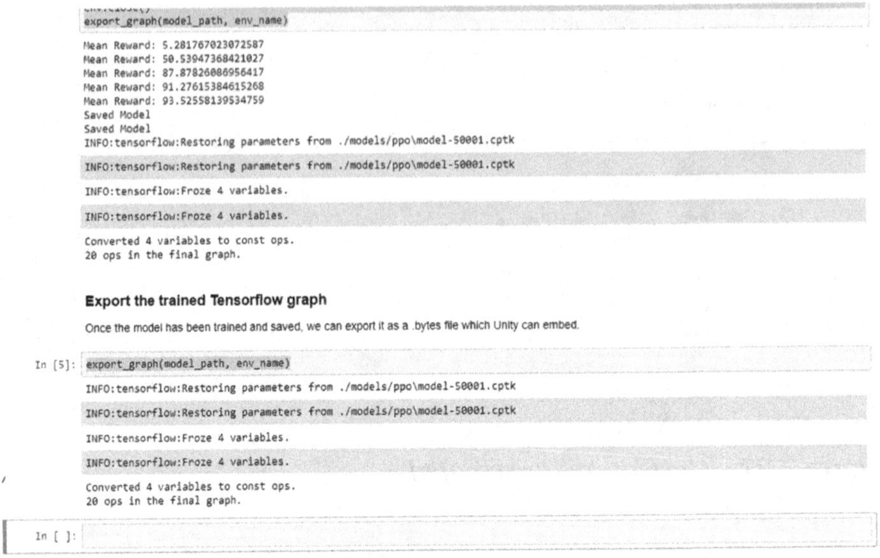

```
export_graph(model_path, env_name)

Mean Reward: 5.281767023072587
Mean Reward: 50.53947368421027
Mean Reward: 87.87826086956417
Mean Reward: 91.27615384615268
Mean Reward: 93.52558139534759
Saved Model
Saved Model
INFO:tensorflow:Restoring parameters from ./models/ppo\model-50001.cptk

INFO:tensorflow:Restoring parameters from ./models/ppo\model-50001.cptk

INFO:tensorflow:Froze 4 variables.

INFO:tensorflow:Froze 4 variables.

Converted 4 variables to const ops.
20 ops in the final graph.
```

Export the trained Tensorflow graph

Once the model has been trained and saved, we can export it as a .bytes file which Unity can embed.

```
In [5]:  export_graph(model_path, env_name)

INFO:tensorflow:Restoring parameters from ./models/ppo/model-50001.cptk

INFO:tensorflow:Restoring parameters from ./models/ppo/model-50001.cptk

INFO:tensorflow:Froze 4 variables.

INFO:tensorflow:Froze 4 variables.

Converted 4 variables to const ops.
20 ops in the final graph.

In [ ]:
```

Figure 2-29. *The TensorFlow graph is exported*

Let us check if the byte file is created or not within the folder (Figure 2-30).

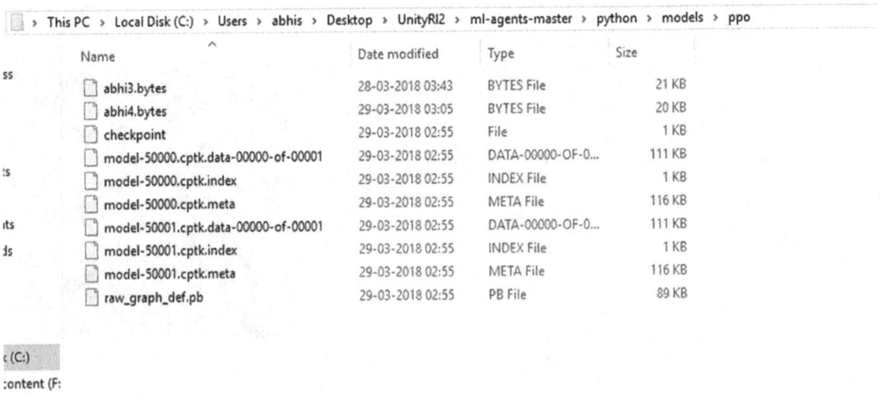

> This PC > Local Disk (C:) > Users > abhis > Desktop > UnityRl2 > ml-agents-master > python > models > ppo

Name	Date modified	Type	Size
abhi3.bytes	28-03-2018 03:43	BYTES File	21 KB
abhi4.bytes	29-03-2018 03:05	BYTES File	20 KB
checkpoint	29-03-2018 02:55	File	1 KB
model-50000.cptk.data-00000-of-00001	29-03-2018 02:55	DATA-00000-OF-0...	111 KB
model-50000.cptk.index	29-03-2018 02:55	INDEX File	1 KB
model-50000.cptk.meta	29-03-2018 02:55	META File	116 KB
model-50001.cptk.data-00000-of-00001	29-03-2018 02:55	DATA-00000-OF-0...	111 KB
model-50001.cptk.index	29-03-2018 02:55	INDEX File	1 KB
model-50001.cptk.meta	29-03-2018 02:55	META File	116 KB
raw_graph_def.pb	29-03-2018 02:55	PB File	89 KB

Figure 2-30. *The bytes file generated needs to be copied*

We will have to copy the abhi4.bytes file to the Unity file folder, but before that we will have to download the TensorFlowSharp plugin (Figure 2-31). It is available in the following link:

`https://github.com/Unity-Technologies/ml-agents/blob/master/`
`docs/Using-TensorFlow-Sharp-in-Unity.md`

TensorFlowSharp is useful for running pretrained TensorFlow graphs in Unity games. We will first import the plugin inside Unity.

Figure 2-31. *Opening the TensorFlowSharp plugin*

Within the edit project settings and then player, we will target the inspector window and check the configuration option that Scripting Runtime Version is Experimental (.NET 4.6 Equivalent).

And within Scripting Define Symbols, we have to enable TensorFlow (Figure 2-32).

Mac App Store Options	
Bundle Identifier	com.Company.ProductName
Version*	1.0
Build	0
Category	public.app-category.games
Mac App Store Validation	☐

Configuration	
Scripting Runtime Version*	Experimental (.NET 4.6 Equivalent)
Scripting Backend	Mono
Api Compatibility Level*	.NET 4.6
Disable HW Statistics*	☐
Scripting Define Symbols*	
ENABLE_TENSORFLOW	
Active Input Handling*	Input Manager

Optimization	
Prebake Collision Meshes*	☑
Keep Loaded Shaders Alive*	☐
▶ Preloaded Assets*	

Figure 2-32. *Enabling the TensorFlow mode*

Now we will copy the bytes we generated to the tfmodels folder (Figure 2-33).

Name	Date modified	Type	Size
3DBall.bytes	01-11-2017 08:38	BYTES File	20 KB
3DBall.bytes.meta	01-11-2017 08:38	META File	1 KB
abhi4.bytes	29-03-2018 03:05	BYTES File	20 KB

Figure 2-33. *The bytes file is being copied to the tfmodels folder*

Within the brain script, we will change the ball type from external to internal.

As we change the ball type to internal, it asks for the missing text asset (Figure 2-34). Here we have to drag and drop the bytes file.

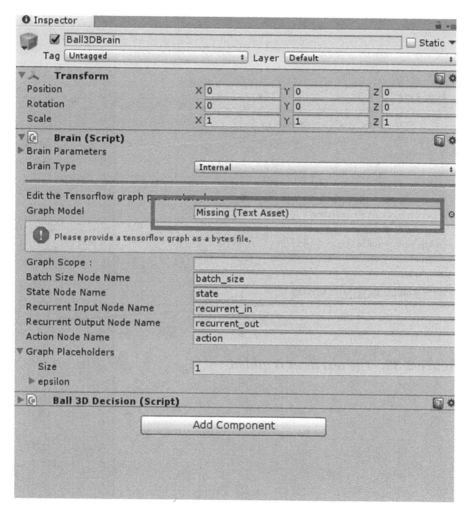

Figure 2-34. *The missing text asset will have to be added*

After adding the bytes file, we will click Run (Figure 2-35).

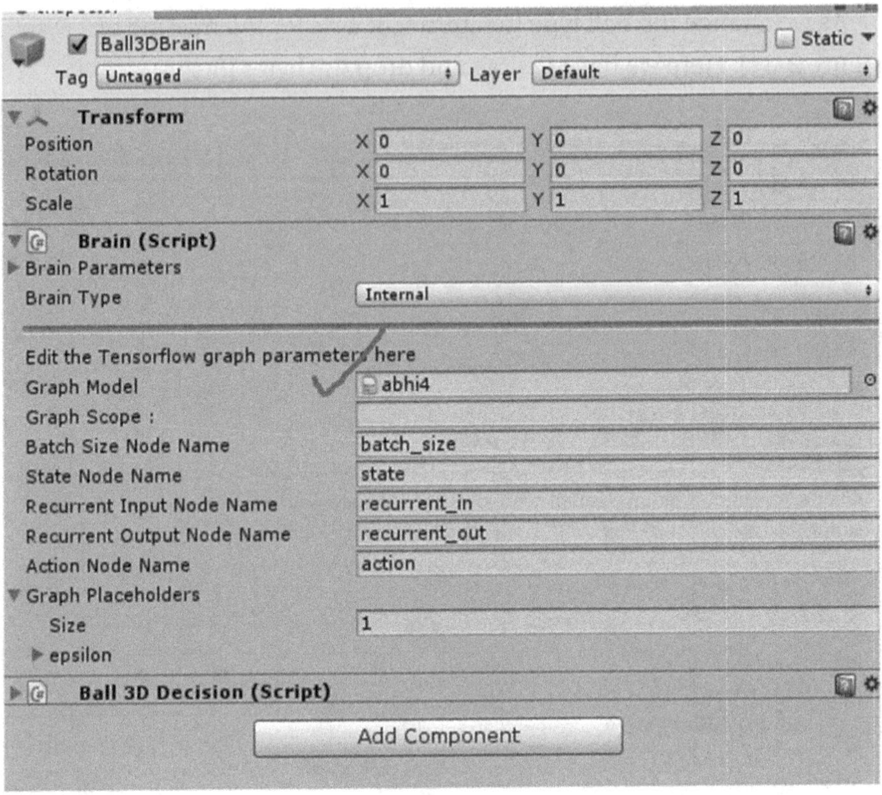

Figure 2-35. *The text asset is added*

You will see now see the MK-Agents trained version running (Figure 2-36).

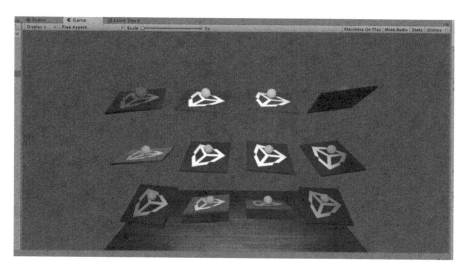

Figure 2-36. *The results after applying ML*

Summary

In this chapter we have touched on the Unity ML-Agents feature. It's one of the important features now enabled in Unity for research purposes. It enables us to do a lot of simulation for different scenarios of our own.

In the chapter we touched on how we downloaded Unity ML-Agents and set it up in Unity. Then we trained the model in Jupyter Notebook. Finally, using PPO, we trained an example already present in the cloned repo.

In the next chapter, we will explore more and also use Neural Networks with Unity.

CHAPTER 3

Machine Learning Agents and Neural Network in Unity

In this chapter we will cover the extended Machine Learning Agents v 0.3 in Unity with an example and then move along to creating a neural network in Unity and adding different assets to it.

First we introduce Machine Learning agents in Unity. Then we will move along with the crawler example in Unity, applying reinforcement learning and comparing both the outputs before training as output from the player and then internally with machine learning agents.

We move along to creating a feedforward neural network in Unity and then getting to know it using Unity output.

Finally we will add the spider animation asset to it and extend the example accordingly.

© Abhishek Nandy, Manisha Biswas 2018
A. Nandy and M. Biswas, *Neural Networks in Unity*,
https://doi.org/10.1007/978-1-4842-3673-4_3

Extending the Unity ML-Agents with Further Examples

In the previous chapter we were focusing on v 0.2 of the ML-Agents, but in this chapter we look at the advanced version 0.3 of the ML-Agents. Let's now download the 0.3 version (Figure 3-1).

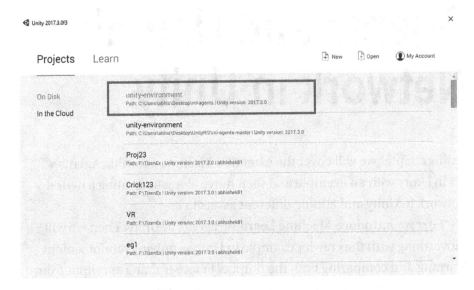

Figure 3-1. *Opening the project*

The unity environment needs to be opened up so that we can take the example project.

Crawler Project

We will work on the crawler example (Figure 3-2).

When we open up the assets folder the Ml-agents we will have a crawler subfolder there and need to open it up in the Unity Game Engine.

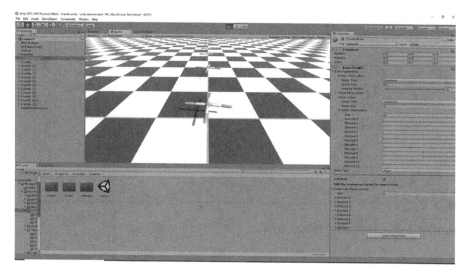

Figure 3-2. *Crawler example*

For simulation purposes, we consider the crawler as a creature with four arms and four forearms.

Goal: The purpose of the simulation is to move the creature on the x axis without falling to the ground.

Now we will save the scene and build the project (Figure 3-3).

Figure 3-3. *Building the project*

We will save the build now.

We need to save the build in a Python subfolder, because we have important files and libraries for running the training for the machine learning agents in this folder (Figure 3-4).

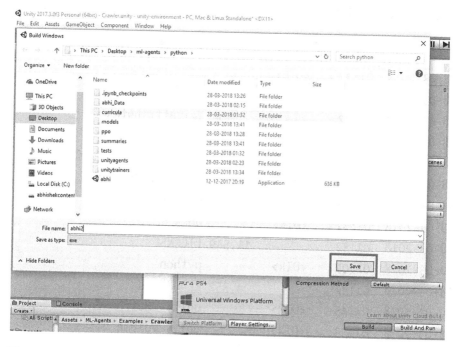

Figure 3-4. *Saving the scene and creating the exe*

Now let us open Anaconda and enable Tensorflow.

We open a command prompt; within there we will write the following command.

```
(C:\Users\abhis\Anaconda3) C:\Users\abhis>activate tensorflow-
gpu
Activate tensorflow-gpu
```

Directory of C:\Users\abhis\Desktop\ml-agents

```
28-03-2018  01:32    <DIR>              .
28-03-2018  01:32    <DIR>              ..
28-03-2018  01:32                   64 .gitattributes
28-03-2018  01:32                1,365 .gitignore
28-03-2018  01:32                3,264 CODE_OF_CONDUCT.md
28-03-2018  01:32                2,519 CONTRIBUTING.md
28-03-2018  01:32                  312 Dockerfile
28-03-2018  01:32    <DIR>              docs
28-03-2018  01:32               11,549 LICENSE
30-03-2018  02:07    <DIR>              python
28-03-2018  01:32                4,352 README.md
30-03-2018  01:45    <DIR>              unity-environment
28-03-2018  01:32    <DIR>              unity-volume
               7 File(s)         23,425 bytes
               6 Dir(s)  30,530,846,720 bytes free

(tensorflow-gpu) C:\Users\abhis\Desktop\ml-agents>cd python

(tensorflow-gpu) C:\Users\abhis\Desktop\ml-agents\python>
```

Let us create a specialized environment for it.

We will set up an environment with Python and Tensorflow (Figure 3-5).

```
Anaconda Prompt - conda  create -n ml-agents python=3.6

(C:\Users\abhis\Anaconda3) C:\Users\abhis>conda create -n ml-agents python=3.6
Fetching package metadata .................
Solving package specifications: .

Package plan for installation in environment C:\Users\abhis\Anaconda3\envs\ml-agents:

The following NEW packages will be INSTALLED:

    pip:            9.0.1-py36_1   conda-forge
    python:         3.6.4-0        conda-forge
    setuptools:     27.2.0-py36_1
    vs2015_runtime: 14.0.25420-0   conda-forge
    wheel:          0.30.0-py36_2  conda-forge

Proceed ([y]/n)? ▄
```

Figure 3-5. *Creating an environment in Anaconda*

After that it starts installing Tensorflow (Figure 3-6).

```
Anaconda Prompt - pip install .
  Downloading enum34-1.1.6-py3-none-any.whl
Requirement already satisfied: wheel>=0.26 in c:\users\abhis\anaconda3\envs\ml-agents\lib\site-packages (from tensorflow==1.4.0->unityagents==0.3.0)
Collecting tensorflow-tensorboard<0.5.0,>=0.4.0rc1 (from tensorflow==1.4.0->unityagents==0.3.0)
  Downloading tensorflow_tensorboard-0.4.0-py3-none-any.whl (1.7MB)
    100% |████████████████████████████████| 1.7MB 671kB/s
Collecting python-dateutil>=2.1 (from matplotlib->unityagents==0.3.0)
  Downloading python_dateutil-2.7.2-py2.py3-none-any.whl (212kB)
    100% |████████████████████████████████| 215kB 2.2MB/s
Collecting cycler>=0.10 (from matplotlib->unityagents==0.3.0)
  Downloading cycler-0.10.0-py2.py3-none-any.whl
Collecting pyparsing!=2.0.4,!=2.1.2,!=2.1.6,>=2.0.1 (from matplotlib->unityagents==0.3.0)
  Downloading pyparsing-2.2.0-py2.py3-none-any.whl (56kB)
    100% |████████████████████████████████| 61kB 1.8MB/s
Collecting kiwisolver>=1.0.1 (from matplotlib->unityagents==0.3.0)
  Downloading kiwisolver-1.0.1-cp36-none-win_amd64.whl (57kB)
    100% |████████████████████████████████| 61kB 1.5MB/s
Collecting pytz (from matplotlib->unityagents==0.3.0)
  Downloading pytz-2018.3-py2.py3-none-any.whl (509kB)
    100% |████████████████████████████████| 512kB 1.3MB/s
Collecting nbconvert (from jupyter->unityagents==0.3.0)
  Using cached nbconvert-5.3.1-py2.py3-none-any.whl
Collecting ipykernel (from jupyter->unityagents==0.3.0)
  Using cached ipykernel-4.8.2-py3-none-any.whl
Collecting jupyter-console (from jupyter->unityagents==0.3.0)
  Using cached jupyter_console-5.2.0-py2.py3-none-any.whl
Collecting qtconsole (from jupyter->unityagents==0.3.0)
  Using cached qtconsole-4.3.1-py2.py3-none-any.whl
Collecting ipywidgets (from jupyter->unityagents==0.3.0)
  Using cached ipywidgets-7.1.2-py2.py3-none-any.whl
Collecting notebook (from jupyter->unityagents==0.3.0)
  Using cached notebook-5.4.1-py2.py3-none-any.whl
```

Figure 3-6. *Installing Tensorflow*

We use the following command to start training the exe we created.

```
python learn.py C:\Users\abhis\Desktop\ml-agents\python\abhi2.
exe --run-id=abhi2 -train
```

The logs are created as it is getting trained.

```
INFO:unityagents:{'--curriculum': 'None',
 '--docker-target-name': 'Empty',
 '--help': False,
 '--keep-checkpoints': '5',
 '--lesson': '0',
 '--load': False,
 '--run-id': 'abhi2',
 '--save-freq': '50000',
 '--seed': '-1',
 '--slow': False,
 '--train': True,
 '--worker-id': '0',
 '<env>': 'C:\\Users\\abhis\\Desktop\\ml-agents\\python\\abhi2.exe'}
INFO:unityagents:
'Academy' started successfully!
Unity Academy name: Academy
        Number of Brains: 1
        Number of External Brains : 1
        Lesson number : 0
        Reset Parameters :

Unity brain name: CrawlerBrain
        Number of Visual Observations (per agent): 0
        Vector Observation space type: continuous
        Vector Observation space size (per agent): 117
        Number of stacked Vector Observation: 1
        Vector Action space type: continuous
        Vector Action space size (per agent): 12
```

Vector Action descriptions: , , , , , , , , , , ,
2018-03-30 02:15:20.293743: W c:\l\work\tensorflow-1.1.0\
tensorflow\core\platform\cpu_feature_guard.cc:45] The
TensorFlow library wasn't compiled to use SSE instructions,
but these are available on your machine and could speed up CPU
computations.
2018-03-30 02:15:21.068815: I c:\l\work\tensorflow-1.1.0\
tensorflow\core\common_runtime\gpu\gpu_device.cc:887] Found
device 0 with properties:
name: GeForce GTX 960M
major: 5 minor: 0 memoryClockRate (GHz) 1.176
pciBusID 0000:01:00.0
Total memory: 4.00GiB
Free memory: 3.35GiB
2018-03-30 02:15:21.076770: I c:\l\work\tensorflow-1.1.0\
tensorflow\core\common_runtime\gpu\gpu_device.cc:908] DMA: 0
2018-03-30 02:15:21.083223: I c:\l\work\tensorflow-1.1.0\
tensorflow\core\common_runtime\gpu\gpu_device.cc:918] 0:   Y
2018-03-30 02:15:21.102662: I c:\l\work\tensorflow-1.1.0\
tensorflow\core\common_runtime\gpu\gpu_device.cc:977] Creating
TensorFlow device (/gpu:0) -> (device: 0, name: GeForce GTX
960M, pci bus id: 0000:01:00.0)
C:\Users\abhis\.conda\envs\tensorflow-gpu\lib\site-packages\
tensorflow\python\ops\gradients_impl.py:93: UserWarning:
Converting sparse IndexedSlices to a dense Tensor of unknown
shape. This may consume a large amount of memory.
  "Converting sparse IndexedSlices to a dense Tensor of unknown
  shape. "
INFO:unityagents:Hypermarameters for the PPO Trainer of brain
CrawlerBrain:
        batch_size: 2024
        beta: 0.005
        buffer_size: 20240

epsilon: 0.2

gamma: 0.995

hidden_units: 128

lambd: 0.95

learning_rate: 0.0003

max_steps: 1e6

normalize: True

num_epoch: 3

num_layers: 2

time_horizon: 1000

sequence_length: 64

summary_freq: 3000

use_recurrent: False

graph_scope:

summary_path: ./summaries/abhi2

memory_size: 256

As we get the training details we also have rewards too (Figure 3-7).

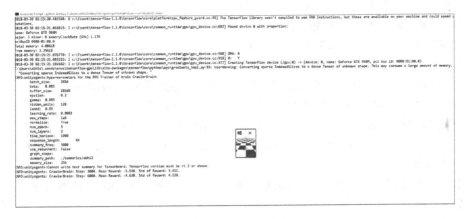

Figure 3-7. *Training started on the crawler model*

We will have to wait for training to be completed.

As we see the saved model being shown, we know a file has been generated (Figure 3-8).

```
time_horizon:    1000
sequence_length:       64
summary_freq:    3000
use_recurrent:   False
graph_scope:
summary_path:    ./summaries/abhi2
memory_size:     256
INFO:unityagents:Cannot write text summary for Tensorboard. Tensorflow version must be r1.2 or above.
INFO:unityagents: CrawlerBrain: Step: 3000. Mean Reward: -5.548. Std of Reward: 3.411.
INFO:unityagents: CrawlerBrain: Step: 6000. Mean Reward: -4.638. Std of Reward: 4.120.
INFO:unityagents: CrawlerBrain: Step: 9000. Mean Reward: -1.258. Std of Reward: 6.745.
INFO:unityagents: CrawlerBrain: Step: 12000. Mean Reward: 3.426. Std of Reward: 8.739.
INFO:unityagents: CrawlerBrain: Step: 15000. Mean Reward: 5.606. Std of Reward: 9.785.
INFO:unityagents: CrawlerBrain: Step: 18000. Mean Reward: 7.461. Std of Reward: 10.296.
INFO:unityagents: CrawlerBrain: Step: 21000. Mean Reward: 10.725. Std of Reward: 10.608.
INFO:unityagents: CrawlerBrain: Step: 24000. Mean Reward: 11.733. Std of Reward: 13.261.
INFO:unityagents: CrawlerBrain: Step: 27000. Mean Reward: 15.888. Std of Reward: 8.796.
INFO:unityagents: CrawlerBrain: Step: 30000. Mean Reward: 19.162. Std of Reward: 9.148.
INFO:unityagents: CrawlerBrain: Step: 33000. Mean Reward: 20.211. Std of Reward: 8.248.
INFO:unityagents: CrawlerBrain: Step: 36000. Mean Reward: 23.095. Std of Reward: 9.550.
INFO:unityagents: CrawlerBrain: Step: 39000. Mean Reward: 27.865. Std of Reward: 13.040.
INFO:unityagents: CrawlerBrain: Step: 42000. Mean Reward: 33.584. Std of Reward: 17.340.
INFO:unityagents: CrawlerBrain: Step: 45000. Mean Reward: 34.968. Std of Reward: 18.354.
INFO:unityagents: CrawlerBrain: Step: 48000. Mean Reward: 37.556. Std of Reward: 18.181.
INFO:unityagents:Saved Model
INFO:unityagents: CrawlerBrain: Step: 51000. Mean Reward: 39.021. Std of Reward: 17.907.
INFO:unityagents: CrawlerBrain: Step: 54000. Mean Reward: 45.406. Std of Reward: 19.278.
INFO:unityagents: CrawlerBrain: Step: 57000. Mean Reward: 63.017. Std of Reward: 40.757.
INFO:unityagents: CrawlerBrain: Step: 60000. Mean Reward: 191.674. Std of Reward: 233.743.
INFO:unityagents: CrawlerBrain: Step: 63000. Mean Reward: 307.939. Std of Reward: 344.752.
```

Figure 3-8. *When the state is saved*

As the model is generated, we now have the bytes file generated (Figure 3-9).

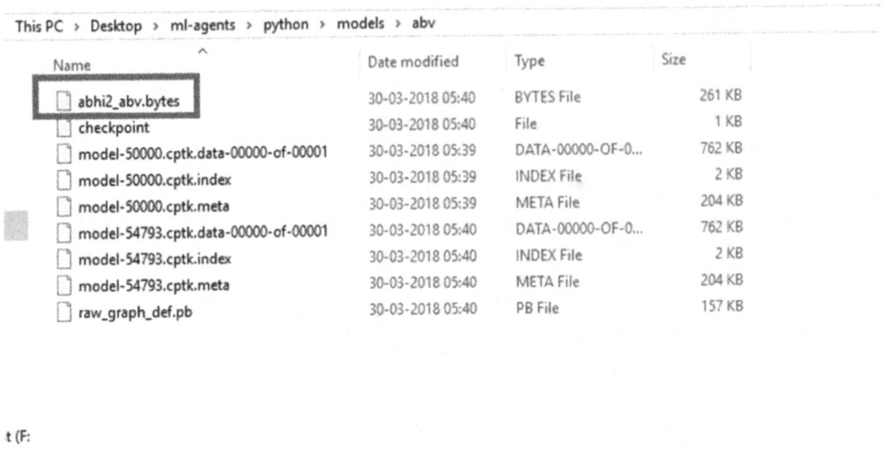

Figure 3-9. *Byte file is created*

Now we will copy the bytes file in the GitHub folder that we have downloaded and opened in the Unity IDE, so it is the same project we are working on. Within the assets folder there will be a TFModels folder. We will copy it there (Figure 3-10).

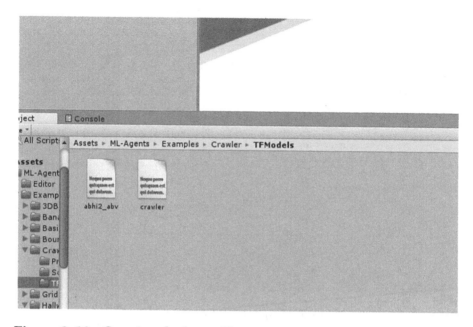

Figure 3-10. *Copying the bytes file in TFModels*

As the bytes file is copied, now we need to change the Brain Type in the inspector window, with the mode being Internal and the byte file generated added as a text asset within Graph Model.

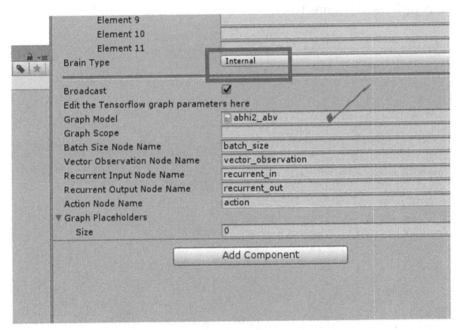

Figure 3-11. *Changing the brain type to internal*

Now let us change certain factors as we have done in the previous chapter. We need to check that in the inspector window within the Configuration option, Scripting Runtime Version is Experimental .net 4.6, and Scripting Define Symbols is set to ENABLE_TENSORFLOW (Figure 3-12).

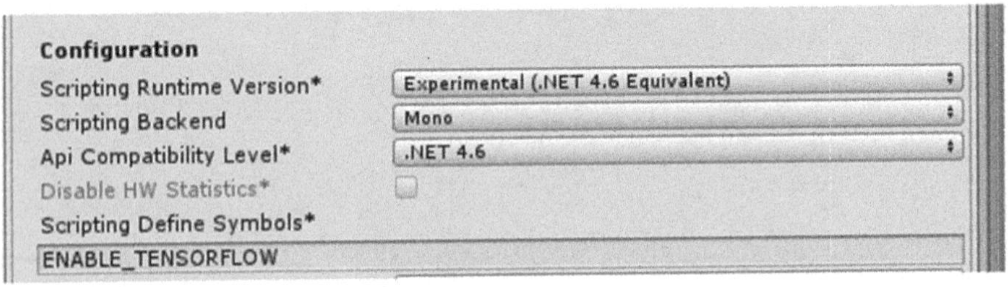

Figure 3-12. *Updating details in configuration*

Testing the Simulation

Let us test the simulation first in player mode, then machine learning mode using internal mode.

When the brain type is player, we see that the output is not perfect (Figure 3-13).

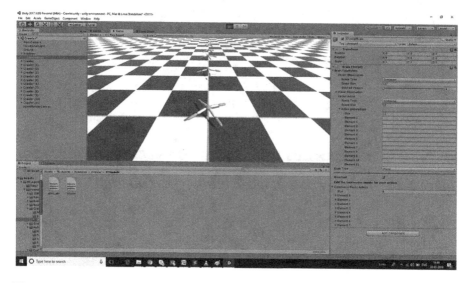

Figure 3-13. *Training output when the brain type is player*

When the brain type is internal, we can see an improvement (Figure 3-14).

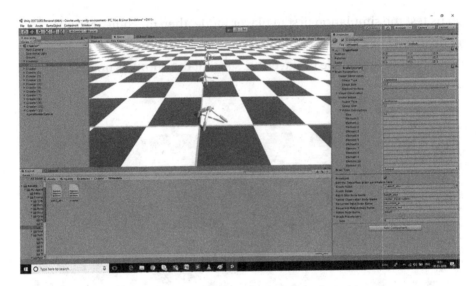

Figure 3-14. *Training output when brain type is internal*

Neural Network with Unity C#

The project that we are trying to create will use 2D capability, so we toggle from 3D to 2D. We name the project NeuralNetwork (Figure 3-15).

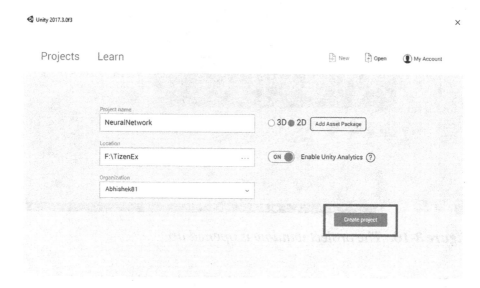

Figure 3-15. *Creating a new project*

The project will open up (Figure 3-16).

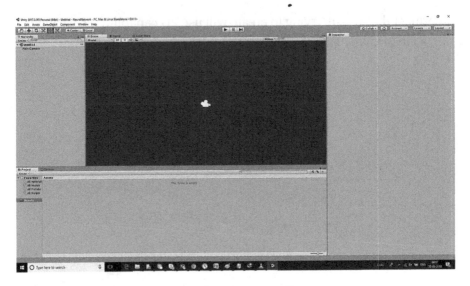

Figure 3-16. *The project window is opened up*

Now we will create two folders, naming one "scene" and the other "script" (Figure 3-17).

Figure 3-17. *Creating folders*

Now we will save the scene in the scene folder. In the file tab we will click save scene and name it as neural.

In the script folder (right click and create a new c# file), we will create a c# file and name it neural network.

The c# file looks like this (Figure 3-18).

```
1  using System.Collections;
2  using System.Collections.Generic;
3  using UnityEngine;
4
5  public class neuralnetwork : MonoBehaviour {
6
7      // Use this for initialization
8      void Start () {
9
10     }
11
12     // Update is called once per frame
13     void Update () {
14
15     }
16 }
17
```

Figure 3-18. *The script file in C# generated*

We will remove everything and the skeleton code will look like this.

```
public class neuralnetwork {

}
```

Now we will create a constructor and name it neural network.

First we need to have some layer array so that we can store the information.

```
private int[] layers;
```

Creating DataStructures

In this section we will work on creating the essential data structures for neurons and the weights associated with them.

Now we will have two data structures: weights and neurons.

We will initialize the layers.

```
public neuralnetwork(int[] layers)
       {
               this.layers = new int[layers.length];
               for(int i=0; i<layers.length; i++)
               {
                       this.layers[i] = layers[i];

               }
               InitNeurons();
               InitWeights();

       }
```

We will also initialize two methods: InitNeurons and InitWeights.

```
       private void InitNeurons()
       {

       }

       private void InitWeights()
       {

       }
```

Now we will create a list and convert it into a jagged array.

We need the jagged array in the neural network because the neural network structure has different flows in one node and in a different node.

```
List<float> neuronsList = new List<float>();

            for (int i = 0; i < layers.length; i++)
            {
                    neuronsList.Add(new float[layers[i]]);
            }
            neurons = neuronsList.ToArray();
```

The preceding code generates the neuron matrix for us.

Now we will create the code for weights.

```
List<float[][]> weightsList = new List<float>([][]);
```

Now we will have to iterate through every single neuron that has a weight connection.

Each layer will need its weight matrix for its neuron, so for this we create a list that contains actual weights of every single neuron.

```
List<float[][]> weightsList = new List<float>([][]);
            for (int i = 1; i < layers.Length; i++)
            {
                    List<float[]> layerWeightList = new
                    List<float[]>();
            }
```

Now we will have a variable as neuronsInPreviousLayer that gives us how many neurons are there in the previous layer.

```
int neuronsInPreviousLayer = layers[i - 1];
```

Now we will iterate through all the neurons in the current layer.

We iterate through all the neurons because if we miss one neuron too, that would result in erroneous output for the entire neural network structure.

```
for (int j = 0;j < neurons[i].Length; j++)
                    {

                    }
```

We will create a neuronWeights, which is the connections of all the neurons that we are targeting, and we will also attach a random weight.

```
for (int j = 0;j < neurons[i].Length; j++)
                    {
                                float[] neuronWeights = new
                                float[neuronsInPreviousLayer]

                                for (int k = 0; k <
                                neuronsInPreviousLayer; k++)
                                {

                                }
                                layerWeightList.
                                Add(neuronWeights);

                    }
```

The updated code after adding random weight is shown as follows.

```
using System.Collections.Generic;
using System;
public class neuralnetwork
{
        private int[] layers;
        private float[][] neurons;
        private float[][][] weights;
```

```
private Random random;
public neuralnetwork(int[] layers)
{
        this.layers = new int[layers.Length];
        for(int i=0; i<layers.length; i++)
        {
                this.layers[i] = layers[i];

        }
        random = new Random(System.DateTime.Today.
        Millisecond);
        InitNeurons();
        InitWeights();

}

private void InitNeurons()
{
        List<float[]> neuronsList = new
        List<float[]>();

        for (int i = 0; i < layers.length; i++)
        {
                neuronsList.Add(new float[layers[i]]);
        }
        neurons = neuronsList.ToArray();

}

private void InitWeights()
{
        List<float[][]> weightsList = new
        List<float>([][]);
```

```csharp
for (int i = 1; i < layers.Length; i++)
{
        List<float[]> layerWeightList = new
        List<float[]>();

        int neuronsInPreviousLayer =
        layers[i - 1];

        for (int j = 0;j < neurons[i].Length;
        j++)
        {
                float[] neuronWeights = new
                float[neuronsInPreviousLayer]

                for (int k = 0; k <
                neuronsInPreviousLayer; k++)
                {
                        neuronWeights[k]
                        = (float)random.
                        NextDouble() - 0.5f;

                }
                layerWeightList.
                Add(neuronWeights);

        }

}

}

}
```

Now we will convert layerweights to 2D jagged array and add it to our weight list.

```
weightsList.Add(layerWeightList.ToArray());
```

We will again convert to 3D weight array.

```
weight = weightsList.ToArray();
```

FeedForward Network

In this section we will see how we apply a feedforward network.

Now we will write a feedforward method for the neural network. We will iterate through the inputs, and add the contents of the input to the first layer of the network.

```
for (int i = 0; i < inputs.Length; i++)
                {
                            neurons[0][i] = inputs[i];
                }
```

Now we are iterating from every single layer, starting from the second layer.

We will now iterate through every single neuron in this layer.

```
for (int i =1; i < layers.Length; i++)
                {
                            for (int j = 0; j < neurons[i].Length;
                            j++)
                            {

                            }
                }
```

We give a value that is a constant bias of 0.25f; it is to be computed from the neuron values, which we will iterate.

```
float value = 0.25f;
```

When we find the value of the weights, it is one item shorter, that is, [i-1] at jth neuron [j] at [k]([i-1][j][k]), multiplying with the values in the previous neuron.

```
value += weights[i-1][j][k] * neurons[i-1][k];
```

We have to pull the value back after applying activation to it.

```
neurons[i][j] = (float)Math.Tanh(value);
```

Now we return the activations.

```
return neurons[neurons.Length -1];
```

We will add a mutate method, which will iterate through all the values on the weight matrix and mutate it based on chance.

```
float randomNumber = (float)random.NextDouble() * 1000f;
```

We will apply four different types of mutation to the weights, based on chance.

```
if (randomNumber <= 2f)
                        {
                                weight *= -1f;
                        }
                        else if (randomNumber <= 4f)
                        {
                                weight = UnityEngine.
                                Random.Range(-0.5f, 0.5f)
                        }
                        else if (randomNumber <= 6f)
```

```
                {
                        float factor =
                        UnityEngine.Random.
                        Range(0f, 1f) + 1f;
                }
                else if (randomNumber <= 8f)
                {
                        float factor =
                        UnityEngine.Range
                        (0f, 1f);
                        weight *= factor;
                }
```

The mutate method is shown as follows.

```
public void Mutate()
        {
                for (int i =0;i < weights.Length; i++)
                {
                        for (int j =0; j < weights[i].Length; j++)
                        {
                                float weight = weights[i][j][k];

                                float randomNumber = (float)
                                random.NextDouble() * 1000f;
                                if (randomNumber <= 2f)
                                {
                                        weight *= -1f;
                                }
                                else if (randomNumber <= 4f)
                                {
```

```
                            weight = UnityEngine.
                            Random.Range(-0.5f,
                            0.5f)
                    }
                    else if (randomNumber <= 6f)
                    {
                            float factor =
                            UnityEngine.Random.
                            Range(0f, 1f) + 1f;
                    }
                    else if (randomNumber <= 8f)
                    {
                            float factor =
                            UnityEngine.Range(0f,
                            1f);
                            weight *= factor;
                    }
                    weights[i][j][k] = weight;

                }
            }
        }
```

Now we will do a deep copy of the network.

```
public NeuralNetwork(NeuralNetwork copyNetwork)
            {
                    this.layers = new int[copyNetwork.
                    layers.Length];
                    for (int i = 0; i < copyNetwork.layers.
                    Length; i++)
                    {
```

```
                    this.layers[i] = copyNetwork.
                    layers[i];
            }

        InitNeurons();
        InitWeights();
        CopyWeights(copyNetwork.layers);

    }
```

We will add a method called copyweights.

```
private void CopyWeights(float[][][] CopyWeights)
        {
                for (int i = 0; i<weights.Length; i++)
                {
                        for (int j = 0; j<weights[i].
                        Length; j++)
                        {
                                for (int k =0; k <
                                weights[i][j].Length;
                                k++)
                                {
                                        weights[i][j][k]
                                        = CopyWeights[i]
                                        [j][k];
                                }
                        }
                }
        }
```

The following is the complete code.

```
using System.Collections.Generic;
using System;

/// <summary>
/// Neural Network C# (Unsupervised)
/// </summary>
public class NeuralNetwork : IComparable<NeuralNetwork>
{
    private int[] layers; //layers
    private float[][] neurons; //neuron matix
    private float[][][] weights; //weight matrix
    private float fitness; //fitness of the network

    /// <summary>
    /// Initilizes and neural network with random weights
    /// </summary>
    /// <param name="layers">layers to the neural network</param>
    public NeuralNetwork(int[] layers)
    {
        //deep copy of layers of this network
        this.layers = new int[layers.Length];
        for (int i = 0; i < layers.Length; i++)
        {
            this.layers[i] = layers[i];
        }

        //generate matrix
        InitNeurons();
        InitWeights();
    }
```

```csharp
/// <summary>
/// Deep copy constructor
/// </summary>
/// <param name="copyNetwork">Network to deep copy</param>
public NeuralNetwork(NeuralNetwork copyNetwork)
{
    this.layers = new int[copyNetwork.layers.Length];
    for (int i = 0; i < copyNetwork.layers.Length; i++)
    {
        this.layers[i] = copyNetwork.layers[i];
    }

    InitNeurons();
    InitWeights();
    CopyWeights(copyNetwork.weights);
}

private void CopyWeights(float[][][] copyWeights)
{
    for (int i = 0; i < weights.Length; i++)
    {
        for (int j = 0; j < weights[i].Length; j++)
        {
            for (int k = 0; k < weights[i][j].Length; k++)
            {
                weights[i][j][k] = copyWeights[i][j][k];
            }
        }
    }
}
```

```
/// <summary>
/// Create neuron matrix
/// </summary>
private void InitNeurons()
{
    //Neuron Initilization
    List<float[]> neuronsList = new List<float[]>();

    for (int i = 0; i < layers.Length; i++)
    //run through all layers
    {
        neuronsList.Add(new float[layers[i]]);
        //add layer to neuron list
    }

    neurons = neuronsList.ToArray(); //convert list to array
}

/// <summary>
/// Create weights matrix.
/// </summary>
private void InitWeights()
{

    List<float[][]> weightsList = new List<float[][]>();
    //weights list which will later will converted into a
    weights 3D array
```

```
//itterate over all neurons that have a weight
connection
for (int i = 1; i < layers.Length; i++)
{
    List<float[]> layerWeightsList = new List<float[]>();
     //layer weight list for this current layer
    (will be converted to 2D array)

    int neuronsInPreviousLayer = layers[i - 1];

    //itterate over all neurons in this current layer
    for (int j = 0; j < neurons[i].Length; j++)
    {
        float[] neuronWeights = new
        float[neuronsInPreviousLayer]; //neruons
        weights

        //itterate over all neurons in the previous
        layer and set the weights randomly between 0.5f
        and -0.5
        for (int k = 0; k < neuronsInPreviousLayer; k++)
        {
            //give random weights to neuron weights
            neuronWeights[k] = UnityEngine.Random.
            Range(-0.5f,0.5f);
        }

        layerWeightsList.Add(neuronWeights); //add
        neuron weights of this current layer to layer
        weights
    }
```

```
        weightsList.Add(layerWeightsList.ToArray());
        //add this layers weights converted into 2D array
        into weights list
    }

    weights = weightsList.ToArray(); //convert to 3D array
}

/// <summary>
/// Feed forward this neural network with a given input array
/// </summary>
/// <param name="inputs">Inputs to network</param>
/// <returns></returns>
public float[] FeedForward(float[] inputs)
{
    //Add inputs to the neuron matrix
    for (int i = 0; i < inputs.Length; i++)
    {
        neurons[0][i] = inputs[i];
    }

    //itterate over all neurons and compute feedforward values
    for (int i = 1; i < layers.Length; i++)
    {
        for (int j = 0; j < neurons[i].Length; j++)
        {
            float value = 0f;

            for (int k = 0; k < neurons[i-1].Length; k++)
            {
                value += weights[i - 1][j][k] * neurons[i -
                1][k]; //sum off all weights connections of
```

```
            this neuron weight their values in previous
            layer
        }

        neurons[i][j] = (float)Math.Tanh(value);
        //Hyperbolic tangent activation
    }
    }

    return neurons[neurons.Length-1]; //return output layer
}

/// <summary>
/// Mutate neural network weights
/// </summary>
public void Mutate()
{
    for (int i = 0; i < weights.Length; i++)
    {
        for (int j = 0; j < weights[i].Length; j++)
        {
            for (int k = 0; k < weights[i][j].Length; k++)
            {
                float weight = weights[i][j][k];

                //mutate weight value
                float randomNumber = UnityEngine.Random.
                Range(0f,100f);

                if (randomNumber <= 2f)
                { //if 1
                  //flip sign of weight
                    weight *= -1f;
                }
```

```
            else if (randomNumber <= 4f)
            { //if 2
              //pick random weight between -1 and 1
                weight = UnityEngine.Random.Range
                (-0.5f, 0.5f);
            }
            else if (randomNumber <= 6f)
            { //if 3
              //randomly increase by 0% to 100%
                float factor = UnityEngine.Random.
                Range(0f, 1f) + 1f;
                weight *= factor;
            }
            else if (randomNumber <= 8f)
            { //if 4
              //randomly decrease by 0% to 100%
                float factor = UnityEngine.Random.
                Range(0f, 1f);
                weight *= factor;
            }

            weights[i][j][k] = weight;
          }
        }
      }
    }

    public void AddFitness(float fit)
    {
        fitness += fit;
    }

    public void SetFitness(float fit)
```

```
{
    fitness = fit;
}

public float GetFitness()
{
    return fitness;
}

/// <summary>
/// Compare two neural networks and sort based on fitness
/// </summary>
/// <param name="other">Network to be compared to</param>
/// <returns></returns>
public int CompareTo(NeuralNetwork other)
{
    if (other == null) return 1;

    if (fitness > other.fitness)
        return 1;
    else if (fitness < other.fitness)
        return -1;
    else
        return 0;
}
}
```

Let us run the application (Figure 3-19).

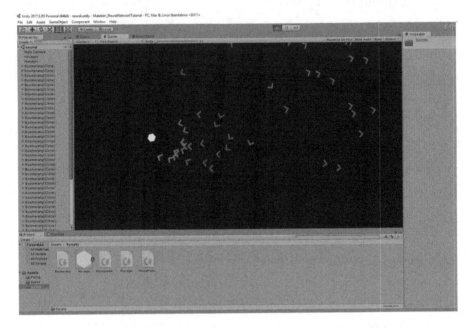

Figure 3-19. *Application running*

Experimenting with the Spider Asset

Let us try the experiment with a different asset; we will use the spider asset.

1. Within the asset store we will find the spider
   animation asset (Figure 3-20).

Figure 3-20. *Adding the spider asset*

2.   We need to import the asset (Figure 3-21).

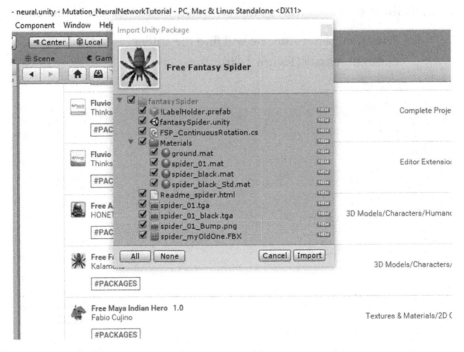

Figure 3-21. *Importing the spider asset*

3. We will drag and drop the spider asset to the scene
    (Figure 3-22).

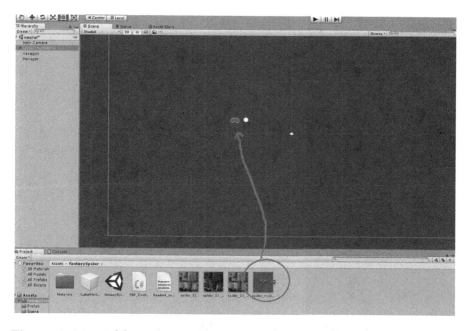

Figure 3-22. *Adding the spider prefab*

4. We rotate the spider using the rotate tool (Figure 3-23).

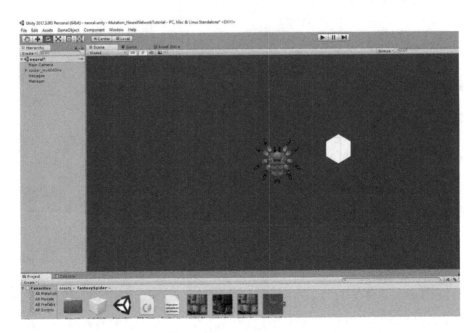

Figure 3-23. *Rotating the spider asset to match*

5. In the Manager in the inspector widow, we add the hex prefab as spider_myOldOne.

6. Add the hexagonAnimator script to the spider_ myOldOne and then click play.

7. We add a mesh renderer to the spider (Figure 3-24).

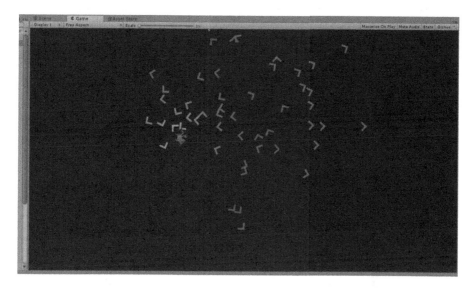

Figure 3-24. *The output*

Summary

In this chapter, we have gone through the details of extending ML-Agents in different environments using an example.

Then we moved along creating a neural network in Unity. Using that, we did one neural network simulation followed by a change in behavior with a different game object.

CHAPTER 4

Backpropagation in Unity C#

In this chapter we will discuss backpropagation with Unity C# and implement accordingly.

As we have already given a brief introduction to backpropagation in the first chapter, in this chapter we will take it further.

We will use an empty Unity project and then start writing a script for backpropagation.

Going Further into Backpropagation

Backpropagation is used to optimize the weights so that the neural network can learn how to correctly map arbitrary inputs to outputs.

In this section we will demonstrate backpropogation with an example (Figure 4-1).

© Abhishek Nandy, Manisha Biswas 2018
A. Nandy and M. Biswas, *Neural Networks in Unity*,
https://doi.org/10.1007/978-1-4842-3673-4_4

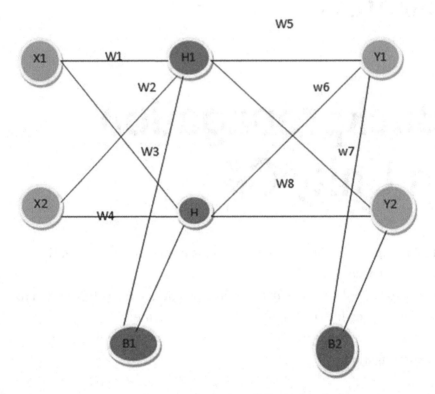

Figure 4-1. *The Neural network that will have backpropagation*

The input from the input layer goes to the hidden layer and then to the output layer, and from the output layer we get the actual output.

Now we will backpropagate the error from the output to the input layer so that we will be updating the weights accordingly.

Let's work on the equation formed by getting the hidden layer.

H1 = X1W1 + X2W2 + b

We will apply a sigmoid activation function to get the output from the hidden layer and also from the output layer.

Sigmoid σ(x) = 1/1+ e-x

Output H1 = 1/ 1 + e-x

Let us assign some values.

X1 =0.05   b1 = 0.35

X2 =0.1   b2= 0.60

Intial weights

W1 = 0.15   W5 = 0.40

W2 =0.20   W6=0.45

W3 = 0.25   W7= 0.50

W4 =0.30   W8 =0.35

Target Values(Output)

T1   T2

0.99

Now we will calculate the forward pass.

H1 = X1W1 + X2W2 + b1

=0.05*0.15 + 0.10*0.20 + 0.35

=0.3775

Out H1 = 1/1+ e-H1 = 1/ 1+e-0.3775 = 0.593269992

In the same way, we derive the Out H2 = 0.596884378

Now we will Calculate Y1.

Y1 = outH1 * W5 +outH2*W6 + b2

=0.4*0.593269992 + 0.596884378*0.45 + 0.6

= 1.105905967

outY1 = 1/1+e-y1 = 1/1+e-1.105905967

= 0.75136507

In the same way, we find Y2.

OutY2 = 0.772928465

The formula for finding the error follows.

Etotal = $\sum$ ½ (target –output)2

=1/2(T1 –OutY1)2 + ½(T2-outY2)2

= ½(0.01-0.75136507)2 + ½(0.99 -0.772)2

=0.274811083 + 0.023560026

=0.298371109

E1 = ½(T1- outY1)2

E2=1/2(T2 –outY2)2

For calculating error we do a backward pass, which is a chained derivate or is a partial differentiation.

This is required to update the weights accordingly.

Consider updating the weight W5.

Error at W5 = ∂Etotal/∂W5

This is partial differentiation.

In the error there is no value for W5. We will use the chain rule for further splitting and getting the desired value.

∂Etotal/∂W5 = ∂outY1/∂outY1 * ∂outY1/∂Y1 * ∂Y1/∂W5

Etotal = ½(T1-outY1)2 + ½(T2-OutY2)2

∂Etotal/∂OUTY1 = 2*1/2(T1-OutY1)2-1 * -1

$\qquad\qquad\qquad$ = -(T1-OutY1)

$\qquad\qquad\qquad$ = -(0.01 -0.75136507)

∂Etotal/∂OUtY1 = 0.74136507

OutY1 = 1/1+ e-Y1

∂outY1/∂Y1 =outy1(1-OutY1)

$\qquad\qquad$ = 0.186815602

∂Y1/∂W1 = 1* OUTH1 * W5(1-1)

$\qquad\qquad$ =OutH1

$\qquad\qquad$ =0.08216704 --→ Change in W5

Now we will be updating W5. We will be using something called learning rate, which is how a neural network leaves the old values and adapts to the change, so we get the updated values for the weights we are looking for at each weight level.

The learning rate always stays between 0 and 1.

Learning rate assigned η

is 0.5 in this example.

W5 = W5 -η* ∂Etotal/∂W5

$\qquad$ =0.4 -0.5 * 0.082167041

W5 = 0.35891648

In the same way, we calculate W6,W7, and W8.

Now at the hidden layer we will update values for W1, W2, W3, and W4.

$\partial \text{Etotal}/\partial W1 = \partial \text{Etotal}/\partial \text{OutH1} * \partial \text{outH1}/\partial H1 * \partial H1/\partial W1$

In the same way, we will calculate the total and get the weighted values, and again update and get the outputs Y1 and Y2. We will iterate backward in the neural until and unless we reduce the error.

- We will discuss important data structures and implement them.

- We will create the complete backpropgation application and test it with an XOR gate.

Let's begin step by step.

Backpropogation in Unity C#

We will apply backpropogation in Unity C#. For that we need to open a new project in Unity (Figure 4-2).

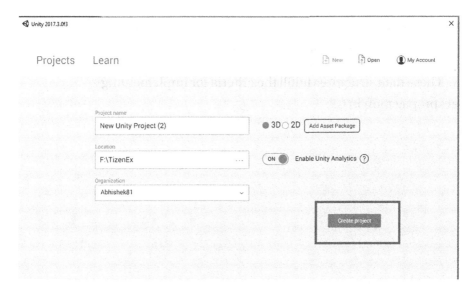

Figure 4-2. *Opening a new project in Unity*

We name the project "backp."

Constructing Data Structures

Before getting in deep, we will be constructing data structures that we will be implementing for backpropogation. First we will have a simple one-dimensional matrix, which will have the output values of any given layer of a neural network.

Float[] output = new float[number of neurons in layer].

Now we will have to have a weight matrix.

```
Float[,] weights = new float[number of neurons in layer, number
of neurons in previous layer]
```

We also need delta values of the weights.

```
Float[,] weightsDelta  = new float[number of neurons in layer,
number of neurons in previous layer]
```

We will gamma the matrix.

```
Float[] gamma =new float[number of neurons in layer]
Float[] error =new float[number of neurons in layer]
```

These data structures fulfill the criteria for implementing backpropagation in C#.

Now we will create a folder within Unity that will contain our C# Script (Figure 4-3).

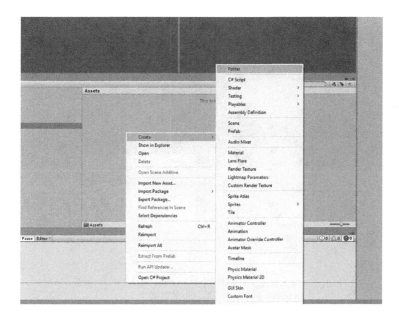

Figure 4-3. *Creating a new C# script*

We will name the folder "script" (Figure 4-4).

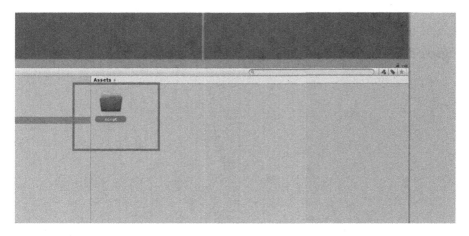

Figure 4-4. *Creating a script folder*

119

Now we will create a new C# script and name it NeuralNetwork (Figure 4-5).

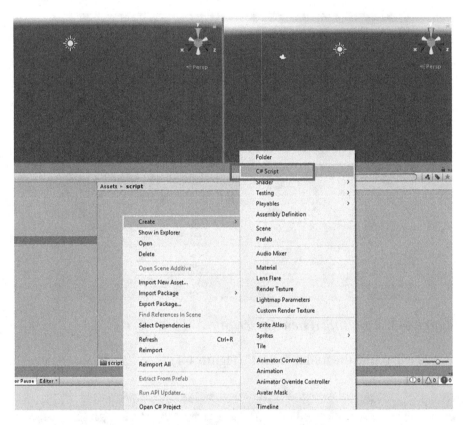

Figure 4-5. *Creating the neural network script*

We will open it up in some editor, in our case Sublime Text (Figure 4-6).

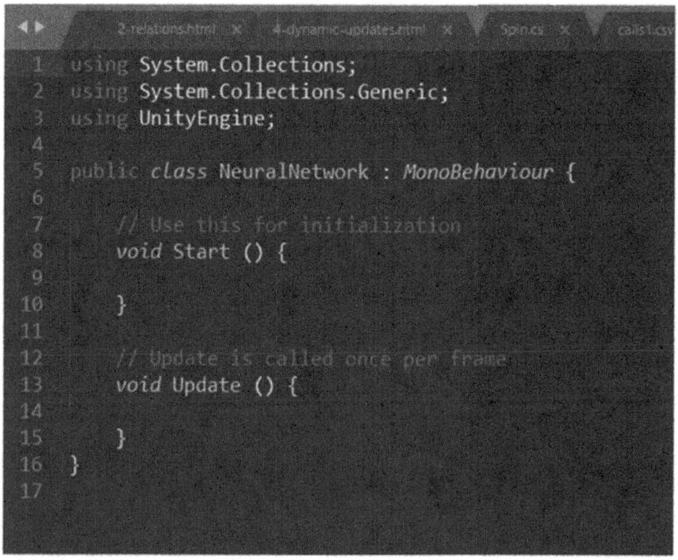

Figure 4-6. *Opening the file in Sublime Text*

We will create a constructor for the neural network.

```
public NeuralNetwork {

    }

    public class Layer {

    }
```

The neural network will take layer information. We will deep copy the layer.

```
public class NeuralNetwork {
    int[] layer;
        public NeuralNetwork(int[] layer)
        {
                this.layer = new int[layer.Length];
                for(int i = 0; i < layer.Length; i++)
                this.layer[i] = layer[i];

        }
```

We will create layer objects.

```
layers = new Layer[layer.length-1]
```

We will work on the layer class now. We will declare the number of neurons in the previous layer as well as the number of neurons in the current layer.

```
public class Layer {
                int numberOFInputs;
                int numberOfOutputs;

                public Layer(int numberOFInputs,
                int numberOfOutputs)
                {
                        this.numberOFInputs = numberOFInputs;
                        this.numberOfOutputs = numberOfOutputs;
                }

        }
```

Now we will declare the data structure in the same manner.

```
float[] outputs;
              float[] inputs;
              float[,] weights;
              float[,] weightsDelta;
              float[] gamma;
              float[] error;
```

We will declare the size of the outputs and inputs.

```
outputs = new float[numberOfOutputs];
inputs = new float[numberOFInputs];

weights = new float[numberOfOutputs, numberOFInputs];
              weightsDelta = new float[numberOfOutputs,
              numberOFInputs];
              gamma = new float[numberOfOutputs];
              error = new float[numberOfOutputs];
```

Feed Forwarding and Initializing Weights

Now we will do feed forward. It will receive an input and feed forward the input. We need to have the last layers of the output values. We have to pass the input in the first layer of the layers.

```
public float[] FeedForward(float[] inputs)
          {
                    layers[0].FeedForward(inputs);
                    for (int i =1; i < layers.Length; i++)
                    {
                              layers[i].FeedForward
                              (layers[i-1].outputs);
                    }
                    return layers[layers.Length -
                    1].outputs;
          }
```

We need to initialize a random number so that we can initialize the weights.

```
public static Random random = new Random();
```

Now we will write a function to initialize the weight.

```
public void InitilizeWeights()
            {
                    for (int i = 0; i < numberOfOutputs; i++)
                    {
                            for (int j =0; j <
                            numberOFInputs; j++)
                            {
                                    weights[i, j] = (float)
                                    random.NextDouble() -
                                    0.5f;
                            }
                    }
            }
```

Now we will write a function that will update the weights for us.

```
public void UpdateWeights()
        {
            for (int i = 0; i < numberOfOuputs; i++)
            {
                for (int j = 0; j < numberOfInputs; j++)
                {
                    weights[i, j] -= weightsDelta[i, j]*0.033f;
                }
            }
        }
```

We subtract from weightsDelta, multiplied by some learning rate.

```
weights[i, j] -= weightsDelta[i, j]*0.033f;
```

We need to add two functions: one is the backpropagation output layer and one is the hidden layer. We need to calculate the derivatives of the error. We will have to write a function that will calculate the derivative of the tanh function.

After updating, the entire code looks like this.

```csharp
using System;

/// <summary>
/// Simple MLP Neural Network
/// </summary>
public class NeuralNetwork
{

    int[] layer; //layer information
    Layer[] layers; //layers in the network

    /// <summary>
    /// Constructor setting up layers
    /// </summary>
    /// <param name="layer">Layers of this network</param>
    public NeuralNetwork(int[] layer)
    {
        //deep copy layers
        this.layer = new int[layer.Length];
        for (int i = 0; i < layer.Length; i++)
            this.layer[i] = layer[i];
```

```
    //creates neural layers
    layers = new Layer[layer.Length-1];

    for (int i = 0; i < layers.Length; i++)
    {
        layers[i] = new Layer(layer[i], layer[i+1]);
    }
}

/// <summary>
/// High level feedforward for this network
/// </summary>
/// <param name="inputs">Inputs to be feed forwared</param>
/// <returns></returns>
public float[] FeedForward(float[] inputs)
{
    //feed forward
    layers[0].FeedForward(inputs);
    for (int i = 1; i < layers.Length; i++)
    {
        layers[i].FeedForward(layers[i-1].outputs);
    }

    return layers[layers.Length - 1].outputs;
    //return output of last layer
}

/// <summary>
/// High level back porpagation
/// Note: It is expexted the one feed forward was done
before this back prop.
/// </summary>
```

```csharp
/// <param name="expected">The expected output form the
last feedforward</param>
public void BackProp(float[] expected)
{
    // run over all layers backwards
    for (int i = layers.Length-1; i >=0; i--)
    {
        if(i == layers.Length - 1)
        {
            layers[i].BackPropOutput(expected);
            //back prop output
        }
        else
        {
            layers[i].BackPropHidden(layers[i+1].gamma,
            layers[i+1].weights); //back prop hidden
        }
    }

    //Update weights
    for (int i = 0; i < layers.Length; i++)
    {
        layers[i].UpdateWeights();
    }
}

/// <summary>
/// Each individual layer in the ML{
/// </summary>
public class Layer
{
    int numberOfInputs; //# of neurons in the previous layer
    int numberOfOuputs; //# of neurons in the current layer
```

```csharp
public float[] outputs; //outputs of this layer
public float[] inputs; //inputs in into this layer
public float[,] weights; //weights of this layer
public float[,] weightsDelta; //deltas of this layer
public float[] gamma; //gamma of this layer
public float[] error; //error of the output layer

public static Random random = new Random(); //Static
random class variable

/// <summary>
/// Constructor initilizes vaiour data structures
/// </summary>
/// <param name="numberOfInputs">Number of neurons in
the previous layer</param>
/// <param name="numberOfOuputs">Number of neurons in
the current layer</param>
public Layer(int numberOfInputs, int numberOfOuputs)
{
    this.numberOfInputs = numberOfInputs;
    this.numberOfOuputs = numberOfOuputs;

    //initilize datastructures
    outputs = new float[numberOfOuputs];
    inputs = new float[numberOfInputs];
    weights = new float[numberOfOuputs, numberOfInputs];
    weightsDelta = new float[numberOfOuputs,
    numberOfInputs];
    gamma = new float[numberOfOuputs];
    error = new float[numberOfOuputs];
```

```csharp
    InitilizeWeights(); //initilize weights
}

/// <summary>
/// Initilize weights between -0.5 and 0.5
/// </summary>
public void InitilizeWeights()
{
    for (int i = 0; i < numberOfOuputs; i++)
    {
        for (int j = 0; j < numberOfInputs; j++)
        {
            weights[i, j] = (float)random.
            NextDouble() - 0.5f;
        }
    }
}

/// <summary>
/// Feedforward this layer with a given input
/// </summary>
/// <param name="inputs">The output values of the
previous layer</param>
/// <returns></returns>
public float[] FeedForward(float[] inputs)
{
    this.inputs = inputs;// keep shallow copy which can
    be used for backpropagation

    //feed forwards
    for (int i = 0; i < numberOfOuputs; i++)
    {
        outputs[i] = 0;
```

```csharp
        for (int j = 0; j < numberOfInputs; j++)
        {
            outputs[i] += inputs[j] * weights[i, j];
        }
        outputs[i] = (float)Math.Tanh(outputs[i]);
    }

    return outputs;
}

/// <summary>
/// TanH derivate
/// </summary>
/// <param name="value">An already computed TanH
value</param>
/// <returns></returns>
public float TanHDer(float value)
{
    return 1 - (value * value);
}

/// <summary>
/// Backpropagation for the output layer
/// </summary>
/// <param name="expected">The expected output</param>
public void BackPropOutput(float[] expected)
{
    //Error dervative of the cost function
    for (int i = 0; i < numberOfOuputs; i++)
        error[i] = outputs[i] - expected[i];

    //Gamma calculation
    for (int i = 0; i < numberOfOuputs; i++)
        gamma[i] = error[i] * TanHDer(outputs[i]);
```

```csharp
    //Caluclating detla weights
    for (int i = 0; i < numberOfOuputs; i++)
    {
        for (int j = 0; j < numberOfInputs; j++)
        {
            weightsDelta[i, j] = gamma[i] * inputs[j];
        }
    }
}

/// <summary>
/// Backpropagation for the hidden layers
/// </summary>
/// <param name="gammaForward">the gamma value of the
forward layer</param>
/// <param name="weightsFoward">the weights of the
forward layer</param>
public void BackPropHidden(float[] gammaForward,
float[,] weightsFoward)
{
    //Caluclate new gamma using gamma sums of the
    forward layer
    for (int i = 0; i < numberOfOuputs; i++)
    {
        gamma[i] = 0;

        for (int j = 0; j < gammaForward.Length; j++)
        {
            gamma[i] += gammaForward[j] *
            weightsFoward[j, i];
        }
```

```csharp
                gamma[i] *= TanHDer(outputs[i]);
        }

        //Caluclating detla weights
        for (int i = 0; i < numberOfOuputs; i++)
        {
            for (int j = 0; j < numberOfInputs; j++)
            {
                weightsDelta[i, j] = gamma[i] * inputs[j];
            }
        }
    }

    /// <summary>
    /// Updating weights
    /// </summary>
    public void UpdateWeights()
    {
        for (int i = 0; i < numberOfOuputs; i++)
        {
            for (int j = 0; j < numberOfInputs; j++)
            {
                weights[i, j] -= weightsDelta[i, j]*0.033f;
            }
        }
    }
}
}
```

Testing of Backpropagation Neural Network

For testing the backpropagation neural network, we need to create a tester that will be an XOR gate trained over 5,000 times (Figure 4-7).

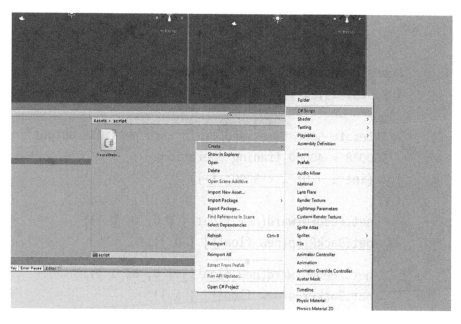

Figure 4-7. *Creating the tester script*

We name it "tester." The XOR will have three values. We have input, hidden layers, and output. It will iterate through more than 5,000 times.

```
using System.Collections;
using System.Collections.Generic;
using UnityEngine;

public class Tester : MonoBehaviour {

        void Start () {
        // 0 0 0    => 0
```

```
// 0 0 1    => 1
// 0 1 0    => 1
// 0 1 1    => 0
// 1 0 0    => 1
// 1 0 1    => 0
// 1 1 0    => 0
// 1 1 1    => 1

NeuralNetwork net = new NeuralNetwork(new int[]
{ 3, 25, 25, 1 }); //intiilize network

//Itterate 5000 times and train each possible output
//5000*8 = 40000 traning operations
for (int i = 0; i < 5000; i++)
{
    net.FeedForward(new float[] { 0, 0, 0 });
    net.BackProp(new float[] { 0 });

    net.FeedForward(new float[] { 0, 0, 1 });
    net.BackProp(new float[] { 1 });

    net.FeedForward(new float[] { 0, 1, 0 });
    net.BackProp(new float[] { 1 });

    net.FeedForward(new float[] { 0, 1, 1 });
    net.BackProp(new float[] { 0 });

    net.FeedForward(new float[] { 1, 0, 0 });
    net.BackProp(new float[] { 1 });

    net.FeedForward(new float[] { 1, 0, 1 });
    net.BackProp(new float[] { 0 });

    net.FeedForward(new float[] { 1, 1, 0 });
    net.BackProp(new float[] { 0 });
```

```
        net.FeedForward(new float[] { 1, 1, 1 });
        net.BackProp(new float[] { 1 });
    }

    //output to see if the network has learnt
    //WHICH IT HAS!!!!!
    UnityEngine.Debug.Log(net.FeedForward(new float[]
    { 0, 0, 0 })[0]);
    UnityEngine.Debug.Log(net.FeedForward(new float[]
    { 0, 0, 1 })[0]);
    UnityEngine.Debug.Log(net.FeedForward(new float[]
    { 0, 1, 0 })[0]);
    UnityEngine.Debug.Log(net.FeedForward(new float[]
    { 0, 1, 1 })[0]);
    UnityEngine.Debug.Log(net.FeedForward(new float[]
    { 1, 0, 0 })[0]);
    UnityEngine.Debug.Log(net.FeedForward(new float[]
    { 1, 0, 1 })[0]);
    UnityEngine.Debug.Log(net.FeedForward(new float[]
    { 1, 1, 0 })[0]);
    UnityEngine.Debug.Log(net.FeedForward(new float[]
    { 1, 1, 1 })[0]);

}


// Update is called once per frame
void Update () {

    }
}
```

We will add this to the main camera and see the output.

Summary

We have covered backpropagation with Unity C#. We have covered the concepts where we introduced the important data structures for the creation of neural network backpropagation.

In Chapter 5 we will be studying a concept of visualizing a dataset in Unity.

We will take example datasets and try to visualize the dataset within a 3D projection in Unity.

CHAPTER 5

Data Visualization in Unity

In this final chapter, we will touch base on how data visualization is implemented in Unity. We conclude the book by visualizing CSV (comma-separated values) data for a good look and feel.

In this chapter, we will start with data visualization and how it is implemented in Unity. As Unity is powered with good GUI options, we can process very rich data for visualization. We start with downloading one open source project from GitHub and modify accordingly. We open the project in Unity and start exploring the options in there. Finally, we create visualizations from CSV files.

Machine Learning Data Visualization in Unity

In this section, we will study how to do data visualization in Unity. Data visualization for ML datasets is very interesting; we will stress that.

© Abhishek Nandy, Manisha Biswas 2018
A. Nandy and M. Biswas, *Neural Networks in Unity*,
https://doi.org/10.1007/978-1-4842-3673-4_5

We will get started with an open source GitHub project (Figure 5-1) and modify it accordingly.

Let's start.

`https://github.com/PrinzEugn/Scatterplot_Standalone`

Figure 5-1. *The open source project*

Now we will have to download it (Figure 5-2).

Figure 5-2. *Downloading the file*

Data Parsing

We will be looking at data parsing in this section. Here we will see how we consume the data from CSV files and use Unity's graphical capability to visualize the dataset.

Before going further, we will touch base on what data we will be parsing. We will be parsing CSV files.

Now, the most important part is the parsing process. We are using a free script that goes through the regular expressions, reads the CSV file, and finally converts it as a dictionary <list> for further usage. The code follows.

In the first section we import the libaries that are required for the project.

```
using UnityEngine;
using System;
using System.Collections;
using System.Collections.Generic;
using System.Text.RegularExpressions;

// Taken from here: https://bravenewmethod.com/2014/09/13/
lightweight-csv-
```

In this section we are declaring a class that intializes the CSV Reader and, using regex expressing, we are going through the dataset and doing the parsing accordingly.

```
reader-for-unity/

// Comments

// Code parses a CSV, converting values into ints or floats if
able, and returning a List<Dictionary<string, object>>.
```

```
public class CSVReader
{
    static string SPLIT_RE = @",(?=(?:[^""]*""[^""]*"")*(?![^""
    ]*""))"; // Define delimiters, regular expression craziness
    static string LINE_SPLIT_RE = @"\r\n|\n\r|\n|\r";

    // Define line delimiters, regular experession craziness
    static char[] TRIM_CHARS = { '\"' };

    public static List<Dictionary<string, object>>
    Read(string file) //Declare method
    {
        //Debug.Log("CSVReader is reading " + file);
        // Print filename, make sure parsed correctly

        var list = new List<Dictionary<string, object>>();
        //declare dictionary list

        TextAsset data = Resources.Load(file) as TextAsset;
        //Loads the TextAsset named in the file argument of the
        function

        // Debug.Log("Data loaded:" + data);
        // Print raw data, make sure parsed correctly

        var lines = Regex.Split(data.text, LINE_SPLIT_RE);
        // Split data.text into lines using LINE_SPLIT_RE
        characters

        if (lines.Length <= 1) return list;
        //Check that there is more than one line
```

```
var header = Regex.Split(lines[0], SPLIT_RE);
//Split header (element 0)

// Loops through lines
for (var i = 1; i < lines.Length; i++)
{
    var values = Regex.Split(lines[i], SPLIT_RE);
    //Split lines according to SPLIT_RE, store in var
    (usually string array)
    if (values.Length == 0 || values[0] == "") continue;
    // Skip to end of loop (continue) if value is 0
```

In this section we are declaring the dictionary object and trimming the characters in the CSV file.

```
length OR first value is empty

        var entry = new Dictionary<string, object>();
        // Creates dictionary object

         // Loops through every value
        for (var j = 0; j < header.Length && j
        < values.Length; j++)
        {
            string value = values[j]; // Set local variable
            value
            value = value.TrimStart(TRIM_CHARS).
            TrimEnd(TRIM_CHARS).Replace("\\", "");
            // Trim characters
            object finalvalue = value;
            //set final value
```

```
            int n; // Create int, to hold value if int

            float f; // Create float, to hold value if float

            // If-else to attempt to parse value into int
            or float
            if (int.TryParse(value, out n))
            {
                finalvalue = n;
            }
            else if (float.TryParse(value, out f))
            {
                finalvalue = f;
            }
            entry[header[j]] = finalvalue;
        }
        list.Add(entry); // Add Dictionary ("entry"
        variable) to list
    }
    return list; //Return list
}
}
```

Let us open the downloaded project (Figure 5-3).

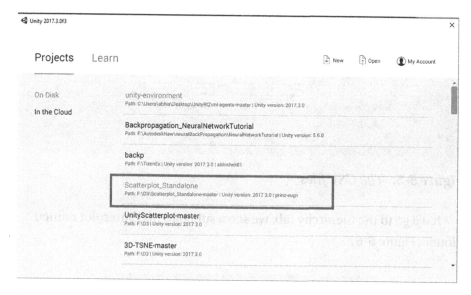

Figure 5-3. *Opening the project in Unity*

The project when opened is shown in Figure 5-4.

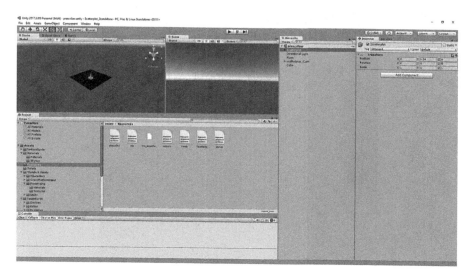

Figure 5-4. *The project windows*

The resources folder will contain all the CSV files (Figure 5-5); you can also add your own files too.

Figure 5-5. *The CSV files*

If we go to the hierarchy tab, we see a subchild of Scatterplot named Plotter (Figure 5-6).

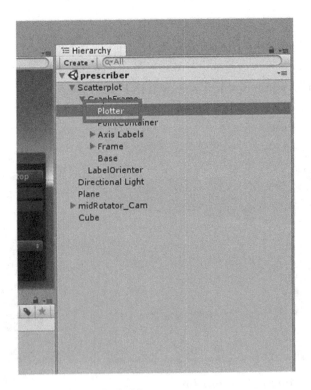

Figure 5-6. *The plotter subchild*

Now, in the inspector window we see the point renderer script. One of the options available is Inputfile, where we can name the CSV file (Figure 5-7).

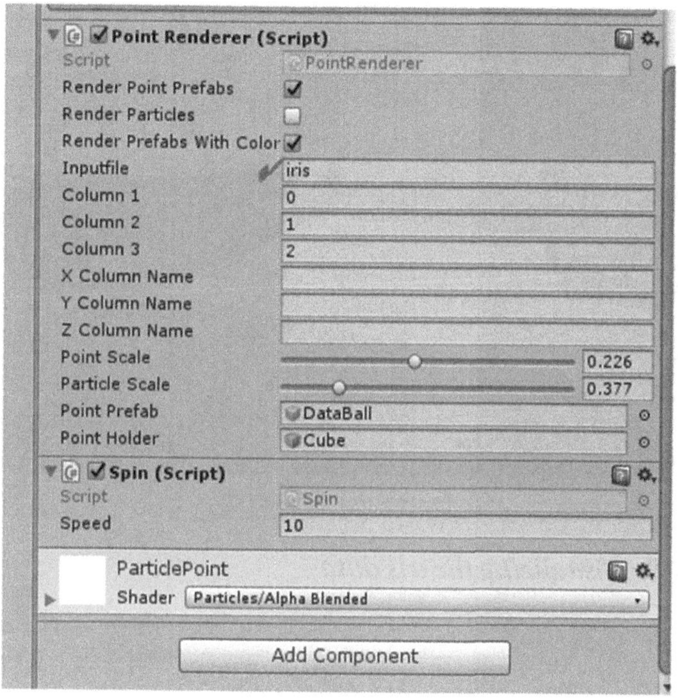

Figure 5-7. *Selecting an input file*

We are using the iris dataset over here (Figure 5-8).

Let's hit the play button to check the visualization.

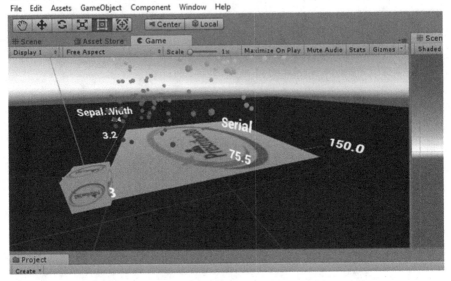

Figure 5-8. *Visualizing the iris data*

Working with Datasets

Let's work on some other datasets.

We open up datagov.in the following address (Figure 5-9).

```
https://data.gov.in/
```

Figure 5-9. *Exploring data.gov.in*

We will work on agriculture data and export it in a CSV file (Figure 5-10).

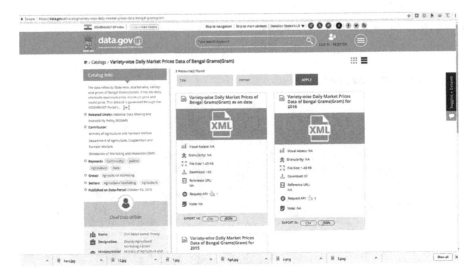

Figure 5-10. *Saving datagov.in data from website*

We use the air quality data and save it (Figure 5-11).

Then we run it.

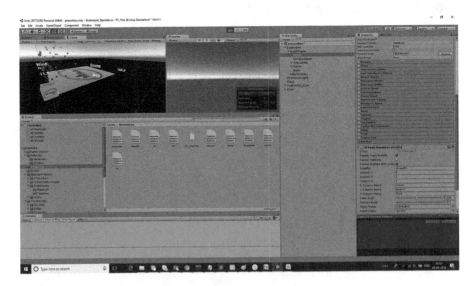

Figure 5-11. *Visualizing the air quality data*

The color effects on the dataset point are added by this part of the script.

```
dataPoint.GetComponent<Renderer>().material.color =
  new Color(x,y,z, 1.0f);
```

Another Example

In this section we will work on another dataset. Let's use it.

We will be using an industrial production dataset (Figure 5-12).

```
https://data.gov.in/catalog/index-industrial-production-0
```

Figure 5-12. *The CSV file that is hosted at datagov.in*

We have saved the file as a CSV format so that the CSV parser is able to parse the information. Let's copy the file in the resources folder.

The file as copied in the resources folder is shown in Figure 5-13.

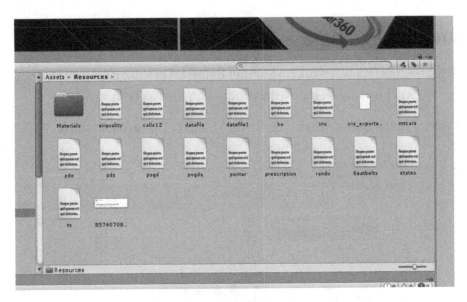

Figure 5-13. *The resources subfolder within the Assets folder*

Now we will work on the CSV file in the inspector window.

In the hierarchy window we see that the plotter is the main field, which contains the CSV input (Figure 5-14).

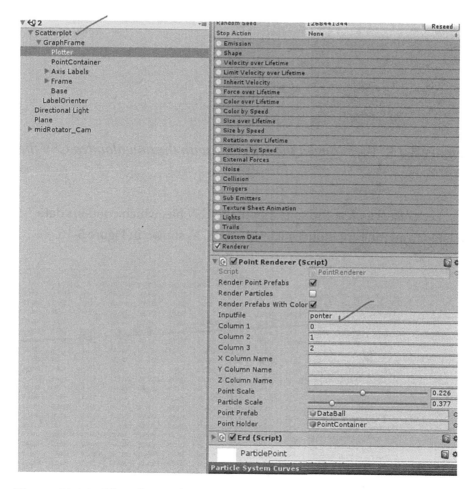

Figure 5-14. *The place where we update the input CSV file*

We will change the input file to read the CSV file we just downloaded from the datagov website. The process as selected from the inspector window is shown in Figure 5-15.

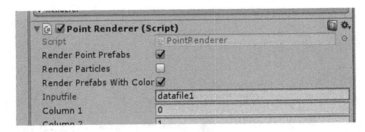

Figure 5-15. *We changed the input file with the downloaded CSV file name*

Let's take a look at the snapshot of the CSV file, which contains data related to an index of industrial production, as shown in Figure 5-16.

A	B	C	D	E	F	G	H	I	J	K	L
Industry code	Description	Weight	2005-2006	2006-2007	2007-2008	2008-2009	2009-2010	2010-2011	2011-12	2012-13	2013-14
15	Food products and beverag	72.76	113.17	131.18	147.52	135.35	133.51	142.87	164.8	169.5	167.7
16	Tobacco products	15.7	101.03	102.88	98.39	102.68	102.03	104.08	109.7	109.2	110.15
17	Textiles	61.64	108.33	116.8	124.57	120.07	127.36	135.87	134	142	148.25
18	Wearing apparel; dressing ;	27.82	114.08	137.19	149.91	134.55	137.12	142.18	130.1	143.6	171.61
19	Luggage; handbags; saddler	5.82	90.87	103.97	109.96	104.36	105.76	114.29	118.5	127.1	133.68
20	Wood and products of woo	10.51	106.84	126.03	148.03	155.28	160.06	156.49	159.2	147.9	144.56
21	Paper and paper products	9.99	106.33	111.01	112.55	118	121.08	131.43	138	138.7	138.62
22	Publishing; printing and rep	10.78	113.68	122.8	140.18	142.36	133.82	148.83	192.8	183	183.41
23	Coke; refined petroleum pi	67.15	100.64	112.58	119.58	123.4	121.75	121.52	125.8	136.4	143.52
24	Chemicals and chemical prc	100.59	101.02	110.43	118.43	114.96	120.73	123.11	122.7	127.3	138.64
25	Rubber and plastics produc	20.25	112.26	119.64	135.68	142.6	167.41	185.21	184.6	185	181.11
26	Other non-metallic mineral	43.14	107.81	119.54	130.63	134.94	145.44	151.37	158.6	161.6	163.3
27	Basic metals	113.35	115.53	132.57	156.32	158.99	162.4	176.69	192.1	195.8	196.43
28	Fabricated metal products;	30.85	111.14	133.31	143.77	143.95	158.59	182.78	203.3	193.8	180.22
29	Machinery and equipment	37.63	126.07	150.93	184.99	170.97	198.04	256.26	241.3	230	219.23
30	Office; accounting and com	3.05	145.33	155.51	164.83	148.82	154.44	146.33	148.7	128.1	108.03
31	Electrical machinery and ap	19.8	116.78	131.56	372.99	530.79	459.18	472.06	367.1	369.2	422.63
32	Radio; TV and communicati	9.89	122.68	312.82	604.16	726.65	809.08	911.48	950.5	1003.7	730.11
33	Medical; precision and opti	5.67	95.35	104.78	111.39	119.77	100.88	107.78	119.5	117.1	111.13
34	Motor vehicles; trailers anc	40.64	110.13	138.04	151.19	138.03	179.11	233.28	258.6	244.8	221.33
35	Other transport equipment	18.25	115.31	132.86	129.01	133.98	171.12	210.74	235.8	235.7	249.5
36	Furniture; manufacturing n	29.97	116.21	111.73	132.67	142.5	152.67	141.18	138.6	131.5	113.27
NA	Mining and Quarrying	141.57	102.27	107.55	112.51	115.4	124.52	131.03	128.5	125.5	124.71
NA	Manufacturing	755.27	110.29	126.79	150.11	153.82	161.25	175.7	181	183.3	181.88
NA	Electricity	103.16	105.16	112.8	119.97	123.26	130.77	138.03	149.3	155.2	164.7

Figure 5-16. *A snapshot of the CSV dataset*

In the columns to project between x, y, and z, we can select years. So let us select 2006-2007, 2011-12, and 2013-14

The columns selections will be numbered from 0 to 11.

We select the first column as 4.

The second column is 9.

The last column is 11.

The inspector view is shown in Figure 5-17.

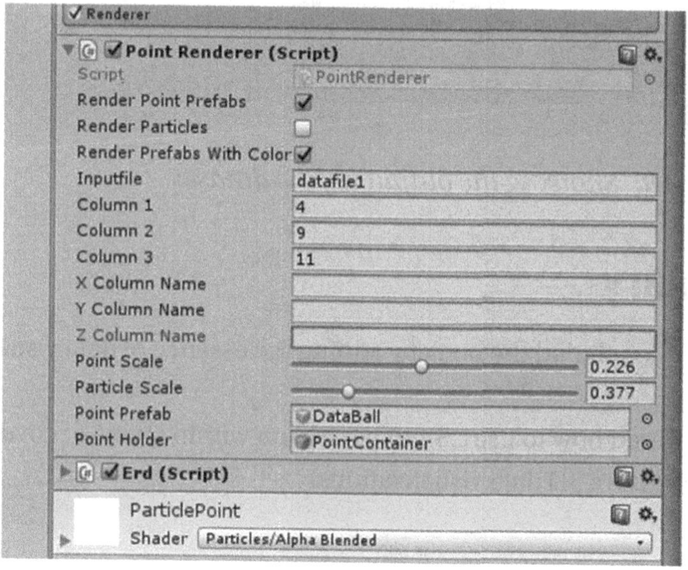

Figure 5-17. Selecting the columns

Now let us run the application and see the output.

The output as achieved is shown in Figure 5-18.

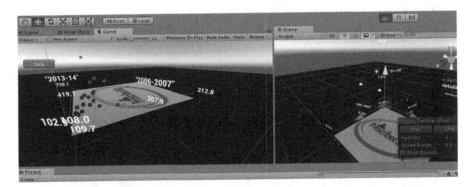

Figure 5-18. *Showing the output for the dataset*

Summary

We hereby concluded the book by adding the essence of data visualization with Unity.

We covered how to use CSV to parse data within Unity, to cover the basic concepts of 3D data visualizations.

Index

A

B

C

D, E, F

G, H

© Abhishek Nandy, Manisha Biswas 2018
A. Nandy and M. Biswas, *Neural Networks in Unity*,
https://doi.org/10.1007/978-1-4842-3673-4

I

Identity function, 7

InitNeurons and InitWeights
methods, 88

Internal operations,
ML-Agents, 44

exe file, 47, 49

inspector window, 46

Jupyter Notebook (*see* Jupyter
Notebook)

ml-agents-master file, 51

player options, 45

Python mode, 49–51

scene and building
selection, 48

J, K

Jupyter Notebook

action_space_type, 54

browser mode, 51

IPython files, 52

matplotlib command, 53

proximity policy
optimization, 57

reward, 56

training mode, 53

Unity file, 55

Unity script, 53

variables and parameters, 56

web browser and appropriate
files, 52

L

Leaky ReLU, 12

Logistic/Sigmoid, 8

M

Machine learning agents
(ML-Agents), 27

Anaconda, 30–34

crawler project (*see* Crawler
project)

GitHub repo, 29

GPU-accelerated TensorFlow

appropriate folder, 37

details, 37

environment, 35

GitHub repo, 35

ml-agents folder, 38

project file, 36

training, 35

unity environments folder, 39

Unity IDE, 38

internal operations (*see* Internal
operations, ML-Agents)

NVIDIA CUDA Toolkit, 34

reinforcement, 28

steps, 28

Tensorflow, 30

unity environment, 70

Unity project

Ball3dBrain, 42

engine opening up, 40

Printed in the United States
By Bookmasters